Ghosts
AND HOW TO
SEE THEM

Ghosts
AND HOW TO
SEE THEM

Peter Underwood

PRESIDENT OF THE GHOST CLUB

BROCKHAMPTON PRESS
LONDON

This book is for
our Rochester, New York friends
CHARLES AND LORRAINE DOERRER
who have walked with us in the steps of
the ghostly Man in Grey in London's
most haunted theatre

First published in Great Britain in 1993
by Anaya Publishers Ltd, Strode House,
44-50 Osnaburgh Street, London NW1 3ND

Copyright © 1993 Peter Underwood
Copyright © 1995 Collins & Brown Ltd

This edition published 1996 by Brockhampton Press,
a member of Hodder Headline PLC Group

Cover photography shows Sandford Orcas Manor House,
Dorset, England (Courtesy Robert Estell)

Frontispiece shows the haunted chapel at Brede Place, Sussex, England,
where bones of a priest were unearthed

Title page shows the 'Demon Drummer of Tedworth' (see p.31)

British Library Cataloguing in Publication Data
Underwood, Peter
Ghosts and How to See Them
I. Title
133.1

ISBN 1 86019 210 6

Designed by Glynn Pickerill
Phototypeset by Art Photoset Ltd, Beaconsfield
Colour reproduction by J. Film Process, Bangkok
Printed and bound in U.A.E.

Contents

PETER UNDERWOOD is the longtime President and Chief Investigator of Britain's Ghost Club and an acknowledged expert on psychic phenomena. He has written several bestselling books on the subject of the supernatural and is a regular worldwide lecturer and broadcaster on all aspects of the unexplained.

Foreword

I have devoted much of my life to the serious and impartial investigation of psychic phenomena and, in particular, to spontaneous psychic activity. None of us is without bias, preconceived opinions, prejudices and partialities, but I have always tried to carry out my investigations with care and objectivity; to listen and not to dismiss anything out of hand simply because people say 'that cannot happen' – a common practice I have found among otherwise distinguished individuals who have been trained to exclude 'irrelevant' considerations from their reasoning.

An open mind is necessary for careful, truthful and objective observation, reasoning and conclusion, and if I have not always achieved such aims, at least I have tried. It has not always been easy to approach the subject with impartiality, but if I have succeeded in opening only one closed mind just a fraction to the very real possibility that objective 'ghosts' do indeed exist, or if only one sceptic decides to seek for himself – to become a ghost hunter – them my journey into these difficult regions will not have been in vain.

Peter Underwood

Savage Club
1 Whitehall Place
London SW1A 2HD

Ghosts

Do They Exist?

'Talking of ghosts, it is wonderful that six thousand years have now elapsed since the creation of the world, and still it is undecided whether or not there has ever been an instance of the spirit of any person appearing after death. All argument is against it, but all belief is for it.' Thus remarked the eighteenth-century English writer, Samuel Johnson, to his friend and biographer, James Boswell. 'This is a question,' he went on, 'whether in theology or philosophy, that is one of the most important that can come before the human understanding.'

'Why are ghosts so fascinating?' researchers have asked through the ages and the answer becomes apparent: 'Because they have always responded to some innate longing in human nature to pierce the veil which hides the future after death.'

'Do you believe in ghosts?' is one of the commonest, but most ambiguous questions which can be asked. But if we take it to mean 'Do you believe that people sometimes experience apparitions?', then the answer is that they certainly do. No one who examines the evidence can come to any other conclusion. Instead of disputing the facts, we must surely try to explain them.

THE EVIDENCE

Ghosts and ghostly activity have been reported from all parts of the world, in every civilization, since the beginning of recorded history. The wealth of available good evidence is quite extraordinary. All kinds of people apparently see ghosts, often only once or twice in a lifetime, but there can be no doubt that on occasions the intelligent and critical as well as the primitive and uneducated of all ages do see them. Overwhelming evidence from widely varied sources and in differing circumstances, climatic conditions and fluctuating degrees of light suggest conclusively that honest people with healthy minds in healthy bodies do see ghosts.

The chances of anyone seeing a ghost during a lifetime are estimated to be as high as one in ten. There are a great many fascinating reports of ghost sightings from the United States, Canada and South America, while the whole of Europe – the British Isles, in particular – has ghost reports that defy rational explanation. The Far East, India, Africa and even Australasia have numerous well-founded ghost stories that have been investigated time and again without a logical explanation for them being discovered. As many experts in the paranormal have asserted, there is simply too much evidence over too wide an area and over too long a time span for it all to be dismissed out of hand.

It is the spontaneous ghost as opposed to the induced ghost of the seance that we are mainly concerned with. Some people regard the forms and figures encountered at seances as 'ghosts', but there is frequently a human element in these materializations which is difficult to separate from the reported entity.

The available evidence suggests that there are many different kinds of spontaneous ghosts, ranging from the historical figures seen repeatedly in haunted historic houses, walking where they walked during their lifetimes and seemingly unconscious of the presence of living human beings or alteration in the structure they once knew, to the recognized ghosts of the recently dead – modern ghosts. If you are in the right place at the right time you will in all probability see a ghost. There are also time slips – visions of a previous time inexplicably reappearing; ghosts of people who have died in traumatic circumstances; happy harmless ghosts of 'something' left behind in the house or grounds they once loved. There are reports of ghosts in daylight; and some especially puzzling cases where a figure has been seen at a particular place on different occasions by people who have no knowledge that such a figure has been seen previously by others. There are indisputably ghosts of animals, and there even seem to be ghosts of inanimate objects and people who are still alive!

Ghosts may vary in degrees of obliquity – from ethereal, almost indistinct shapes bearing little resemblance to a human form, to dense, solid and seemingly real figures that may even block out whatever they pass in front of, as a living person would. So tangible do such figures appear to be that witnesses have been known to address them, and even to reach out to touch them. Only when their hands pass through the ghost without meeting any resistance (and the ghost often abruptly disappears) do the witnesses realize that it is not a real person. But there is no good evidence of spontaneous ghosts speaking.

By the same token ghosts will often appear suddenly and unexpectedly and as suddenly and mysteriously disappear or pass through a solid wall, a closed door or panelling that may have been built or erected after the lifetime of the person represented by the ghost. Thus the ghostly figure is walking and moving within a different dimension from that of the living witness; certainly they are rarely aware of a witness or anything that person does or says.

Almost everyone loves a ghost story, whether it is fictional or, apparently, true. And almost everyone who has had a personal 'psychic' experience – or knows someone who has had such an

experience – is prepared to accept the possibility that some people do see ghosts. In this book I seek to answer the important question: do these things really happen? What is the evidence for them and who are the witnesses? If they do happen, are they paranormal or do they fall into the natural order of things? What are the real chances of anyone seeing a ghost? Where are the most likely places and when is the most likely time?

The problem of ghosts is a very real one, a very ancient one and one that is being addressed almost every day. On the one hand there is the scoffer, the outright sceptic who will not believe anything that he cannot see and touch, or that is not accepted by the scientific establishment. On the other stands the credulous, uncritical and not infrequently unbalanced person who takes practically every odd or out-of-the-way incident that he cannot at once explain as being of paranormal origin, and probably the work of 'spirits'. In between are the serious psychical researchers, the men and women who examine impartially and consider objectively such incidents as are brought to their notice and who try to find out exactly what is happening, and why, and under what conditions – but only after first exploring all possible natural and normal possibilities. There are also a growing number of scientists who do not scoff and (unlike some of their colleagues) say such things do not happen because they cannot

THE AUTHOR beside the haunted mill at Boscastle in Cornwall, England, where there is the ghost of a one-eyed man – a miller who died amid rumours of murder. Sometimes he bends over sleeping occupants, sometimes he is seen walking through a wall in the basement. Other disturbances here have included the sound of heavy footsteps, lights being switched on when the building was unoccupied and doors opening and closing by themselves. Once an occupant went down to the basement and found that the whole area had become a working mill again! A second later everything was as normal

happen. After all, not so many years ago who would have thought we would be able not only to hear, but also to see, someone speaking on the other side of the world? And which one of us has ever seen an x-ray, for example, or a radio wave, but we accept such things exist because we see, and cannot deny, the results.

I and, I hope, the majority of my readers belong somewhere between the two extremes – perhaps not psychical researchers, but people who are sufficiently open-minded to accept the possibility that we may not yet know everything and who are prepared to explore objectively reported paranormal activity.

THE SOMBRE, shadowy and echoing entrance to Harlaxton Manor, in Lincolnshire, England, a Victorian dream palace where I once spent a night in the haunted Clock Room. Ghosts here include the eccentric Violet Van der Elst and an unrecognized dark-robed figure; the screams of a murdered child have also been heard

THE CINEMA OF TIME

The question of whether ghosts exist and, if so, why, was once considered by a member of the Society of Antiquaries in London who saw, at close quarters, the ghost of a Bronze Age horseman. Mr R C C Clay was an acknowledged authority on prehistoric Britain, and was also trained in medicine and science. He subsequently explained his theory as to why some people seem to see some ghosts while others do not. His views have been regarded by many people as a logical explanation for some spontaneous ghosts.

Dr Clay saw the ghost when he was in charge of some excavations being carried out by the Society of Antiquaries on the Late Bronze Age 'urnfield' at Pokesdown near Bournemouth on the Dorset coast. Each day he would drive down to the site and return home in the late afternoon across Cranborne Chase and the Wiltshire Downs.

One day, as he was driving home along the straight road that cuts the open downland between Cranborne and Sixpenny Handley, he noticed a horseman travelling in the same direction. He had reached a spot between a small clump of beeches on his right and a pinewood on his left, where the road dips, when he noticed the horseman turning the horse's head and galloping hard, as though attempting to reach the crossroads ahead first and perhaps force the archaeologist to stop. Clay was so interested that he changed gear to slow the car down so that

A WOODED corner of Cranborne Chase, southern England, where the ghost of a Bronze Age horseman was seen

they would indeed meet, and he thought to himself he would then be able to see the rider and his mount at close quarters. However, before they drew level the horseman turned his horse's head again and galloped parallel with the motorist at a distance of about fifty yards.

By now Dr Clay could see that this was no ordinary horseman. For one thing his legs were bare and he wore a long and loose form of cloak. The horse had a long mane and tail but, peer as he might, the curious observer could not see any bridle or stirrup. The rider's face was at times turned towards Clay yet he found he could not distinguish any features. At times the horseman seemed to be threatening in his behaviour and he would wave some kind of implement or weapon above his head.

To his amazement Dr Clay realized that he was looking at a prehistoric man and he manoeuvred his car to drive at the same speed and as close as possible to the figure to see whether he could perhaps identify and date the implement or weapon. After travelling more or less parallel for perhaps one hundred yards the rider and horse suddenly disappeared. Dr Clay stopped his car and carefully noted the spot where the disappearance had taken place. He found traces of a low, round prehistoric barrow or grave-mound that he had never noticed before.

Many times afterwards when he passed that way, at all times of the day, Dr Clay was alert and looking for the horseman, but he never saw him again. His enquiries, however, produced an old shepherd and two girls who had also seen the figure in the same place on different occasions. The shepherd said the ghost was well-known in the area and always vanished suddenly near 'a low, round barrow'; he said he had seen it himself several times.

Clay believed that certain happenings in life: murder, suicide, accidental death, extreme agony of mind or infinite love and kindness, *can* leave an impression on what he described as 'the cinema of time'. The result is that at relevant periods the episodes of the past are thrown up and repeated on, say, the anniversaries of the happening. He also felt that only some people have the power to see such ghosts since they possess extra-sensory perception, a sixth sense which enables them to see happenings denied to others; and horses, dogs and certain other animals have this sixth sense, too, he believed.

GHOSTS REMEMBERED

I often discussed the subject of memory with my friend Paul Tabori, a Doctor of Philosophy at a university in Budapest, Hungary. He regarded memory as a most unreliable faculty and he told me that it had been established that in relation to any happening only those details which have caught our attention in a decisive instant of time are retained in our memory, quite regardless of their importance or triviality. This, apparently, is the explanation of the gaps and contradictions in the evidence of different witnesses describing the same event.

Often, it seems, it is the deep impression of an event which etches only this or that single phase into memory. Certain states of excitement, fear, expectation, hope and despair have a decisive influence on the receptive powers of the intellect; so that we either sense the facts wrongly or quickly forget even correctly observed circumstances. In the same way suggestion, both during an experience and in its reproduction, can be an important factor. This suggestive falsification of memory, and the adjustment of memory, play a considerable part in many stories concerned with ghosts and ghostly happenings and with prophetic dreams and telepathy, and must always be taken into consideration by investigators.

But these limitations apply only to the functions of our conscious memory. Psychoanalysis has shown that in our subconscious we store numerous sensual impressions which have never penetrated into the full light of the conscious and they emerge repeatedly in dreams, under hypnosis and in sudden inspirations and ideas.

While conscious memory is unreliable, the subconscious memory is clear and exact. It seems that our subconscious memory retains all our experiences with complete faithfulness to the end of our lives, a faculty

that has been called, with some justification, 'absolute memory'. So-called 'total recall' is, of course, impossible, for this 'absolute memory' is not governed by the conscious mind.

HALLUCINATIONS AND DREAMS

The study of philosophy and psychology might help to provide an answer to some stories of ghosts because hallucinations and pseudo-hallucinations may produce identical reactions. For example, a super-stitious peasant could experience a sensory hallucination of seeing his dead son and believe he was seeing the boy's ghost. If the man visited a local sorcerer or wizard who hypnotized him and told him he could see his son, the consequence would be the same whether genuine sensory hallucination had taken place, or whether the sorcerer merely convinced him by suggestion that he had seen his son. In either case the report would go round the neighbourhood that the man in question had seen his son's ghost.

So-called 'collective hallucination' or illusion is sometimes a contributing factor in the emotional excitement at the time of an occurrence. In his book called *Hallucinations and Illusions* E Parish

SCUDAMORE AT Letchworth Corner, Hertfordshire, England, has reportedly been haunted by ghostly footsteps for many years. The disturbances are thought to be associated with the man who had the 300-year-old cottages converted into the present house. One occupant told me that her dog rushed panic-stricken from an apparently empty room and nothing would persuade him to re-enter it. An example of a dog's sixth sense?

13

FREDERIC WILLIAM Myers
(1843-1901). He was a
pioneer of organized
psychical research, a
classical scholar of
outstanding ability and
author of a monumental
work on survival of bodily
death. He wrote an article
about Sir Edmund
Hornby's apparition in
which even he came to the
wrong conclusion

gives an example of this. He relates the case of the whole crew of a
vessel being frightened one evening by what they took to be the ghost
of a cook who had died some days previously. 'He was distinctly seen
by all, walking on the water with a peculiar limp which had
characterized him, one of his legs being shorter than the other. The
cook, who had been recognized by so many, turned out to be a piece
of wreckage, rocked up and down by the waves.' Sceptics suggest this
tale well illustrates the manner in which many stories of ghostly
apparitions receive their genesis.

All ghosts, it has been said, can be dismissed as optical illusions,
delusions or dreams. While this is simply not true, it has to be admitted
that even the most intelligent psychical researcher often finds it difficult
to avoid putting leading questions, or simply fails to ask the right
questions, thus coming to the wrong conclusion. Even people like
Edmund Gurney and F W H Myers (a president of the London

Society for Psychical Research), early psychical researchers of considerable repute, were culpable in this respect and more than once they had to retract what they had presented to the world as 'well-authenticated evidence'. Their article on Sir Edmund Hornby's apparition is a case in point. Of course everyone who has studied the subject has come across cases of ghosts that are not ghosts, but Sir Edmund Hornby was a Chief Judge of the Indian Supreme Court and Gurney and Myers' article publicized a remarkable personal experience nine years after the event.

One night, the Judge records, he heard a tap at his bedroom door, and a certain newspaper editor, with whom the Judge was well acquainted, walked in. He ignored the Judge's requests to leave the room and sat down at the foot of the bed. The time, Sir Edmund noted, was twenty minutes past one. The purpose of the newspaper editor's visit was to obtain a statement from the Judge concerning the day's judgement, for the morning paper. After refusing twice, Sir Edmund gave him the information for fear that further argument would wake Mrs Hornby. Finally, the Judge angrily told his visitor that it was the last time he would allow any reporter inside his house. The other replied: 'This is the last time I shall ever see you anywhere.'

When he had gone, the Judge looked at the clock: it was exactly half past one. Lady Hornby then awoke and the Judge told her what had happened. Next morning Judge Hornby repeated the story to his wife while dressing. When he arrived in court he was somewhat shocked to hear that his visitor of the night before had died during the night – at about one o'clock. In the dead man's notebook was the headline: 'The Chief Judge gave judgement this morning in the case to the following effect . . . ' and then followed some lines of indecipherable shorthand. The result of the inquest showed that the newspaper editor had died of some form of heart disease. The coroner, at the Judge's request, ascertained that the dead man could not have left his house during the two hours before he died.

When he got home the Judge asked his wife to repeat what he had told her during the night and he 'made a brief note of her reply and of the facts'. The Judge added: 'As I said then, so I say now – I was not asleep, but wide awake. My memory is quite clear on the matter. I have not the least doubt I saw the man and have not the least doubt that the conversation took place between us.' Gurney and Myers published a résumé of Sir Edmund Hornby's full and detailed account and Lady Hornby confirmed the facts, 'as far as she was cognizant of them'.

But others looked into the facts and Gurney, Myers and Sir Edmund were in for a shock. Four key facts in the story were found to be inaccurate: (1) The editor in question was the Rev. Hugh Lang Nivens. The actual time of his death was nine o'clock in the morning. (2) At that time Judge Hornby was unmarried. His wife had died two years previously and he did not remarry until three months after the editor's death. (3) No inquest was held on the death of the Rev. Hugh Nivens. (4) There was no record of any such judgement as the Judge mentioned and upon which the whole story turned.

Judge Hornby, when faced with the facts, commented: 'If I had not believed, as I still believe, that every word of it, the story, was accurate, and that my memory was to be relied on, I should not have ever told it as a personal experience.'

There is no need to assume that the story was consciously fabricated. It is sufficient to think that a good deal of it was the product of a vivid dream which was later confused with reality, and rationalized and elaborated during subsequent conversations. It might be regarded as a fairly typical case of retrospective falsification.

PHYSICAL REALITY

Yet more than a few people have become convinced of the objective reality of ghosts after personal inquiry. One author, Anne Bradford, set out to compile a book devoted to the ghosts in and around her home town, Redditch, Worcestershire in England's midlands, and when she began Mrs Bradford was really sceptical, she tells me, and thought she would 'just get a few quaint stories of stately homes'. Now she is 'not so sure' about the reality of ghosts, having listened to so many strange stories 'from the most reliable of people'.

Anne Bradford was not the first person to notice one interesting feature: a person who sees one ghost is likely to see a second; and she soon realized that the number of people who do see ghosts, or who honestly think they see ghosts, is quite remarkable. She found the common problem was not to locate people who had seen ghosts but to persuade those people to talk about their experiences. It could be that the experience was so horrific or so frightening or so seemingly inexplicable that they just wanted to forget it, but the majority were afraid of public reaction and the opinions of their friends, neighbours and relatives.

Some psychical researchers had little time for seeking to establish the reality of a haunted house using scientific equipment and scientific-minded observers. The late Charles Seymour, an English researcher, was one. All he would take to a haunted house, he used to say, was 'a first-class medium' and then he would 'persevere' until they learned who or what the ghost really was. Leaving on one side for a moment who decides a medium is 'first-class' and where such an individual is to be found, the idea may be worthy of serious consideration.

If a 'psychic' is able to 'tune in' to psychic activity more acutely than an ordinary mortal, it seems reasonable to take such a person on a haunted house investigation; but who decides what directions and undertakings to follow and how much reliance to place on any information obtained? If past records are anything to go by, uncheckable, informal, involuntary and uncorroborated testimony

concerning unknown people and places is likely to be forthcoming; material similar to that sometimes obtained at seances. By no stretch of imagination can such information be regarded as scientific or worthy of serious consideration by unbiased witnesses.

Nevertheless Seymour, in particular, had what he called a psycho-physical theory which did not necessarily involve the hypothesis of a spirit world nor, indeed, need such a world necessarily be regarded as supernormal since we are a long way from defining the boundaries of the 'normal', physiological and psychological, in our own world. He believed that a large number of well-attested 'hauntings' can very reasonably be explained on a 'physical' theory, by which he meant that on what we know as matter there can be, and are, recorded impressions of events that have occurred in its presence and that, under suitable conditions, these events 'can again become dynamic'.

He suggested as a parallel the gramophone record or disk, our 'crude earth way of recording sounds'. A record, or a cassette or compact disc could be 'haunted' by the sound recorded upon it for as long as the

THE CHURCH of St Bartholomew the Great, Smithfield, London, has long been haunted by the ghost of its twelfth-century founder, Rahere, a monk-courtier to Henry I. The ghost has reportedly been seen on many occasions in the vicinity of Rahere's tomb, and witnesses include a former rector, the Rev. F G Sandwith (who saw the ghost twice), four actors, during a rehearsal of a nativity play in 1932 and, more recently, the historian Dorothea St Hill Bourne, who saw the shadowy form while singing in the church

shellac or tape lasts. In view of the historical evidence that nature has preceded so many of man's inventions, it could be thought odd if nature were less clever than ourselves in failing to provide a similar sensitivity which can preserve sights and sounds under certain conditions. With the passing of time it may be that the 'recording' dims and eventually disappears – or perhaps, an intriguing thought, those who witness the sights or sounds so recorded somehow 'feed' the haunting so that the more a haunting is witnessed the longer it lasts. Of course not everyone is able to witness these 'phenomena', and possibly the presence of people who do not see ghosts acts against the preservation of the 'haunting', which might all but disappear, perhaps only slight sounds or indistinct forms persisting.

This rerunning of stored impressions or events could be described as nature's equivalent of a cinematic film, rather like Clay's 'cinema of time', an idea that adequately explains some hauntings, but only some. Those who favour such a theory suggest that psychic power, or a force unconnected with living human beings, becomes concentrated and localized at a certain place where the occupants, or the people who live nearby, or those who visit, act as a trigger that releases the pent-up force from the surrounding physical field and its stored-up impressions become tangible and manifest.

At least one investigator has suggested that a rough analogy would be to scatter through a house many small iron and steel objects, and then for a person wearing a suit of armour that has been highly magnetized to walk through the house. The movement and disturbances that would ensue among the small metal objects would be comparable to the phenomena that occur when certain persons reside or visit a haunted house where psychic power is stored; a difference in the strength and intensity of the disturbances being due to the degree of 'magnetization' or the psychic content of the human being present.

Whatever the explanation everyone loves a 'true' ghost story and can tell you an anecdote that defies logical explanation from their own life or from an impeccable source. But an anecdotal story, however detailed and seemingly convincing, has no scientific worth unless it can be investigated, analysed and dissected. This is very rarely possible, practicable or feasible but the accumulative total of so much well-attested experience must surely count for something.

It may well be that man has always had a need for mystery and the unknown to give him a meaning to life – and that may have been the origin of religion, for example. Certainly convincing tales of super-natural happenings cater for a deep-seated need in mankind, but they cannot be the whole answer. If only a minute percentage of the millions of ghost stories is fact – indeed, if only *one* is factual – then we are all faced with enormous problems in our present-day attitude to evolution, time, matter, space, death and even life itself. To paraphrase Voltaire: if ghosts did not exist it would be necessary to invent them.

Ghosts

SPOT THE DIFFERENCE

Ghosts mean different things to different people: frightening figures of fun; odd incidents experienced by friends; wispy forms in shadowy ruins; evidence of an after-life; spirit forms of dead people; indistinct figures in the dim atmosphere of a seance-room; or illusions that other people have – to mention a few. It is not always appreciated that those who have studied the subject are aware that there appear to be many different kinds of spontaneous ghosts. Let us look at some of these ghost categories and the evidence for them.

HISTORICAL GHOSTS

These are the ghostly figures that are supposed to haunt old houses and there is hardly a large or small house of any appreciable age that does not have a ghost, or the reputation for having one.

Glamis Castle, the Queen Mother's Scottish home, has a dark, uncertain history. It is centuries old, massive, pinnacled, brooding and mysterious, with great grey granite turrets. It may well have been

INSIDE SCOTLAND'S most haunted house, Glamis Castle, where there are a dozen ghosts and many secret rooms and mysteries

haunted when Shakespeare wrote *Macbeth* and it was probably the scene of the murder of Duncan by Macbeth, Thane of Glamis – and, if so, his was only one of several violent deaths said to have sullied this fairy-tale building.

The ghosts here include the cruel 'Earl Beardie', possibly in reality the first fifteenth-century Lord Glamis whose old rooms are haunted to this day; and a Tongueless Woman, said to have been seen by 'many' people over the years. There is also a ghostly Lady in White who walks the dim corridors at night and a little black boy who sits outside the Queen Mother's sitting-room; while the nearby dressing-room is haunted by unexplained sounds and the movement of objects.

THE HAUNTED library at Blickling Hall in Norfolk, England

HENRY VIII'S queen, Anne Boleyn, may have lived in an earlier house on the site of Blickling Hall, where she is alleged to haunt. Her ghost has also been seen at Hampton Court Palace, Hever Castle, Salle Church, Rochford Hall, Bollin Hall and Windsor Castle

More evidence than exists for any of these phantoms, however, is available for a Grey Lady who haunts the tiny chapel. The last Lord Strathmore, the 17th Earl, told me he had seen the Grey Lady several times; the present Queen Mother and her sister, the late Lady Granville and many others also claim to have seen this quiet ghost who may be Janet, Lady Glamis, wife of the sixth Lord Glamis, who was burned alive at Edinburgh, the capital of Scotland, more than four hundred years ago.

Then, apart from reputed ghosts, there are at Glamis the locked and secret rooms. The last time I was there Lord Strathmore told me he was certain that there were undiscovered human remains somewhere within the massive walls and 'probably half-a-dozen bricked-up rooms. . .'. There are still many mysteries to be solved at Glamis and all its dark and uncertain history will probably never be revealed.

At some historic English houses the alleged haunting is slight. For example beautiful Blickling Hall in Norfolk has long been reputedly haunted by the ghost of Anne Boleyn, the unfortunate second wife of Henry VIII, who may have lived for a time in an earlier house on the

GOODWOOD HOUSE in Sussex, England, is reputedly visited by a phantom coach and horses

site, and by the ghost of her father Sir Thomas Boleyn, once a year. Christina Hole, a prominent member of the English Folklore Society, writing in 1940, says, 'the occupants of the house are so used to this annual appearance that they take no notice of it'. In 1984 the Custodian told me: 'The likeness of Anne has been seen walking in the gardens by the lake.' But persistent and reliable evidence for any haunting here is unconvincing.

Similarly Goodwood House, the seat of the Duke of Richmond and Gordon, in Sussex is reputedly haunted by a phantom coach and horses. This arresting sight was seen by two witnesses about fifty years ago, but reliable and recent evidence is very thin on the ground. Perhaps this is an example of a ghostly appearance that has gradually faded over the years, and finally disappeared.

Longleat House in Wiltshire – home of the Marquess of Bath and now famous for its lions – has been described as the most haunted stately home in England. It has a ghostly Green Lady; the phantom form of Sir John Thynne, who built the immense mansion and is the recognized head of the line; Bishop Ken, whose ghost annually returns to the Library he so loved; the murdered Thomas Thynne; two unidentified ghosts, one in a small room in the house and another in the Stable Courtyard; and ghost swans. To this impressive list the late Marquess of Bath added for me the ghost of Cardinal Wolsey, Henry VIII's Chancellor, riding in a phantom coach; a mysterious 'man in grey'; and the ghost of a Cavalier, who supported the King in England's Civil War. Certainly residents and many visitors affirm that Longleat is indeed haunted.

Springhill, a splendid manor house in Co. Londonderry, Northern Ireland, is described by an information officer in Ireland as 'our most celebrated haunted house'. In common with many genuine ghost-infested houses the paranormal activity centres on the staircase, in this case a broad and substantial oak structure, where the ghostly figure of a tall woman has been seen, sometimes on the stairway but more often at the top of the stairs. The ghost of a small, squat woman dressed all in black was also seen at the foot of the stairs.

There is a haunted room, too, where George Lenox Conyngham took his own life. He was a descendant of the Colonel Conyngham who acquired the house in the seventeenth century. Objects have moved without being touched by human hand and several articles have completely disappeared; and a phantom form has been seen, standing by the fireplace. Other reported happenings here, which do not appear to have any rational explanation, include the sounds of wrangling and whispering, as though the room is full of people; a curious clicking noise, and the sound of marching and stamping feet.

Then there is the 'White Lady of Berlin', who allegedly haunted the Old Palace at the end of the Unter den Linden avenue there for three hundred years. The palace was built by the cruel Frederick Hohenzollern, Elector of Brandenburg, who became the first King of Prussia in 1701; and he used an Iron Maiden instrument of torture inside the infamous Tower of the Green Hat. The well-authenticated ghost does not seem to be one of these victims, however, although there are those who maintain that the White Lady was the model for the awful Iron Maiden, but she is a beautiful woman who apparently reappeared many times after her death to warn the descendants of King Frederick of their own approaching ends. Others believe she is the ghost of an early Hohenzollern, Countess Agnes of Orlemunde, who murdered her two children, a ghost who became known as the 'White Lady of the Hohenzollerns'. The ghost at the Old Palace was

HAUNTED SPRINGHILL in Co. Londonderry – Northern Irelands's 'most celebrated haunted house'

first reported in 1719, and was immediately associated with a royal death. Subsequently she is said to have been seen by, among others, King Frederick William II in 1792; by Prince Louis of Prussia in 1806; by Napoleon Bonaparte when he was staying at the Old Palace; and by Kaiser Wilhelm II in June 1914; while in April 1945 she was seen again as Berlin burned. After the Second World War the Old Palace, damaged but not impossible to repair, was destroyed by the Russians.

These traditional or historical ghosts appear to be solid, they act naturally and are seemingly dressed in clothes of their time. In common with practically all spontaneous ghosts they never speak and rarely show any sign of being aware of the presence of human beings. Often they have suffered in some way during their earthly life and they may well have a kinship with the Atmospheric Photograph Ghost (see below) since they are place-centred, confined in the main to ancient properties or ruins, perhaps reinforcing the idea that stones can store emotions, impressions and, in particular, tragic events, and they apparently continue for centuries.

THE OLD Palace stood on the Unter den Linden in Berlin but was destroyed by the Russians after the Second World War. It was the haunt of the White Lady of Berlin for over 300 years. This phantom form was reputed to herald a royal death

ATMOSPHERIC PHOTOGRAPH GHOSTS

These are ghosts (sometimes called Mental Image Ghosts) reported from all parts of the world over many years, that suggest that certain events – often, but not always, tragic or violent events – occasionally imprint themselves in or on the atmosphere of the place or area where the events occurred, resulting in something like a cinema film appearing to anyone who happens to be in the right place at the right time. These ghosts are only visible from a certain viewpoint and they are always doing the same thing – as indeed they must, for they are 'photographic' recordings of past events.

Interestingly enough, when they are first seen they exactly resemble the past event, with accompanying sounds, but with the passing of the years the visual aspect gradually fades as the figures become transparent and eventually nothing is visible. But the sounds remain until, again after some years, they fade, too, almost like a battery running down. Psychic animals such as horses and dogs may still show an awareness of 'something' at the scene of the one-time haunting, as may psychically-gifted people.

THE SPECTACULAR coloured statue of Captain Coke, reputedly murdered by his own brother to obtain an inheritance in 1632, is said to come to life on certain nights of the year and to step down from the monument and run round the interior of this fine Devon church at Ottery St Mary. The origin of the legendary story of a running ghost is unknown, but there are theories suggesting that certain ghostly manifestations run down after a period, almost like a battery, and then, although visual aspects disappear, any aural attributes remain. Interestingly enough, there have been a number of reported incidents of unexplained running footsteps at night inside this church

It may be that the climate plays a part in this curious recording system for these events seem to remain as light-particles, imprinted and vibrating for years in the same place. I have noticed, for instance, that such ghost 'imprints' are rarely reported in exposed places where high winds are frequent, and it may be that such conditions inhibit the process necessary for such recordings.

A well-known example of this type of manifestation, an interior one, is the seemingly well-established ghost of Queen Catherine Howard, Henry VIII's fifth wife, at Hampton Court Palace just outside London.

The story goes that on 4 November 1541 the Queen escaped from her guards after she had been arrested at the Palace and rushed towards the chapel to make a last appeal for her life to the King, only to be taken back, sobbing for mercy and shrieking with terror, when the King piously continued his worship, pretending he did not hear her. She was then imprisoned in her room, which she only left when she was taken to the Tower for execution in February 1542.

THIS POSTCARD was sold at Hampton Court Palace. It shows a simulated ghost of Queen Catherine Howard

Catherine and Henry lived and loved and enjoyed each other's company in various rooms and apartments of Hampton Court; but nothing of that remains. There are just the frantic screams of the terrified young Queen as she rushed along what has become known as the Haunted Gallery. This traumatic event somehow became impressed on the atmosphere of the place and has occasionally been re-enacted ever since. The screams, in particular, have been reported by many of the residents and not a few have glimpsed a figure in white, with loose, flying hair, rushing along the same panelled gallery. For years the Palace shop sold postcards depicting the event.

HAMPTON COURT Palace, once the home of King Henry VIII, is reputedly haunted by screaming Catherine Howard, silent Jane Seymour, blue-clad Anne Boleyn, stately Cardinal Wolsey and a mysterious Lady in White

CYCLIC OR RECURRING GHOSTS

The appearance of the screaming ghost of Queen Catherine Howard seems not to have any rhythm or pattern, but other ghosts, triggered by equally traumatic occurrences, recur in regular cycles, usually annually, and they are known as Cyclic or Recurring Ghosts.

It is almost as though whatever is necessary to cause such ghosts to appear takes a set time, say exactly twelve months, to build up again. Reported cyclic ghosts are numerous but few are well-authenticated, and it may be that the presence of certain people or a certain type of person, climatic conditions, atmospheric pressure and alterations in the magnetic fields may all play a part in such periodic manifestations. (See the Ghost Calendar on p97.)

Well-known cyclic ghosts in England include 'a white shape' in the vicinity of the Bloody Tower at the Tower of London each 12 February, the anniversary of the execution of Lady Jane Grey, who was made Queen of England for ten days in 1553; a drummer boy seen on Hickling Broad, Norfolk, each 15 February; the annual reappearance of 'Juliet', who hanged herself on 17 March in the vicinity of the Ferry Boat Inn, Holywell, Cambridgeshire; the ghostly form of Lady Blanche de Warren each 4 April at Rochester Castle, Kent, where she was killed by an arrow on that day in 1264; a phantom coach which drives towards Blickling Hall in Norfolk each 19 May and then vanishes; another phantom coach which crashes into the old bridge at Potter

Heigham in the same county at midnight each 31 May; a phantom sailor who is seen in Ballyheigue Bay, Ireland, each 4 June; a ghost Cavalier who visits Hitchin Priory in Hertfordshire each 15 June; the famous ghost nun who walks each 28 July at Borley Rectory in Essex; the ghost of Sir Walter Raleigh who returns to his old home, Sherborne Castle in Dorset, each 28 September; Costania, Lady Coleraine, who manifests each 3 November at Bruce Castle, Tottenham, in London, where she committed suicide; and a 'grey lady' who walks at the Royal National Orthopaedic Hospital, Stanmore, London, each 13 November. In December, Christmas Eve and the last day of the year are positively bursting with ghostly activity. On the former Anne Boleyn walks again at Hever Castle in Kent; a ghost monk wanders among the ruins of Strata Florida Abbey in Dyfed, Wales; a phantom coach and horses visits Roos Hall, Beccles, in Suffolk; the ghost of Charles Dickens wanders about the graveyard in the shadow of Rochester Castle; and a bell rings from the depths of

THE WAKEFIELD Tower, in the Tower of London – perhaps the most haunted collection of buildings anywhere in the world

HITCHIN PRIORY in Hertfordshire, England, is reputedly visited each 15 June by the ghost of a Cavalier named Goring who, wounded in a skirmish during the English Civil War, sheltered in a house called High Down at nearby Pirton. He was discovered and killed. His ghost has apparently been sighted within the last few years

Bomere Pool near Shrewsbury in Shropshire. While on 31 December King John's hounds appear at Purse Caundle Manor in Dorset; a ghost carriage crosses the frozen Loch of Skene, west of Aberdeen in Scotland; a spectral pig appears at Andover in Hampshire; and a black horse races out of the drive at Ranworth Old Hall, Norfolk.

Group cyclic manifestations include a phantom, silent army which appears on the shores of Loch Ashie near Inverness in Scotland each 1 May at dawn. This is the site of an ancient battle between the defending Gaelic Fionn (or Fingal) and the men of Lochlann (Norway) led by King Ashie.

In the case of cyclic ghosts, more than any other psychic manifestation, it is perhaps necessary to bear in mind the power of the human mind, for if we visit somewhere that we know is reputed to be haunted by a certain figure on a certain day, we are half-way towards seeing such a figure before we even get there!

ROCHESTER CASTLE, Kent, England, where a ghost known as the White Lady has haunted for more than 700 years. She is thought to be Lady Blanche de Warren, who was accidentally killed by her betrothed, Ralph de Capo. That night her ghost walked the battlements where she died and she has been seen periodically ever since. The Old Burial Ground, situated in the castle moat, is also haunted – on Christmas Eve – by the ghost of Charles Dickens, who expressed a wish to be buried in this little graveyard

FAMILY GHOSTS

These are ghosts that for some peculiar reason attach themselves to certain families. Often, it seems, their function is to warn the family of impending disaster or a family death. In some cases the manifestation is non-human, in others it is the appearance of a former family member; in others again it is not an appearance but something that affects a physical object or the appearance of a seemingly physical object – the falling of a picture and the guttering of a candle were once common manifestations of family ghosts, for example. On many occasions priests and exorcists have attempted to lay family ghosts, be

they phantom drummers, phantom riders, phantom birds or phantom people. The result has always been the same: no effect, and the haunting goes on, as if the family ghost will continue to manifest as long as there remains any member of the haunted family.

Among the doom-laden English families haunted by ghost birds are the Oxenhams of Devon, famous for the white bird which for centuries foretold a death in the family. A white bird was first seen in 1618 in the chamber where old Mother Oxenham died. Then her grandson John was unexpectedly taken ill in 1635 and died within a few days. As he lay dying a bird with a white breast was seen to hover about him. Within days Thomazine, John's sister-in-law, suddenly fell ill and died, and again a white bird was seen in the death chamber. The same sickness soon killed two infant members of the family and on each

LEWTRENCHARD HOUSE in Devon, England, was once the family home of the Baring-Goulds and has long been haunted by the eighteenth-century Margaret Baring-Gould. A little girl visitor here saw the ghost of 'a dear old lady in old-fashioned dress' in the so-called Haunted Gallery; the ghost has also been seen in her favourite place, sitting beside the fireplace in the present drawing-room, and in the garden

occasion a white bird appeared, although no bird was seen in the vicinity of other members of the family who recovered from the same illness.

Through the seventeenth century and right up to the nineteenth century, when the Oxenhams left their ancestral home, the inexplicable appearance of a white bird heralded the death of an Oxenham. It was seen in locations ranging from Kensington to Canada and legend has it that such a bird even fluttered over the head of one Margaret Oxenham during her wedding some 200 years ago, when she was suddenly confronted by a rejected lover who stabbed her to death at the altar.

The prestigious Arundel family from Wiltshire were for centuries aware of the appearance of two white owls, usually seen on the roof of their ancestral home, just before the death of someone in the family. The family died out in 1944. The Caldwells, an ancient family from the centre of England, had – and perhaps still have – a phantom bird of brilliant plumage that appeared prior to a death in the family. This individual 'bird' has been seen by friends and visitors as well as by family members, but only hours later, after the death of a Caldwell, would the family reveal that the appearance of such a bird heralded a death.

Other family ghosts in the form of animals include a ghost bat (the Moxey family from the Midlands) and a black calf (the Shirley family from Staffordshire); while prophetic family ghosts in human form include the mysterious Red Man who manifests to members of the Bonaparte family; a monk (the Henderson family from Warwickshire); a nun (the Middletons of Yorkshire); and then there are ghostly White Ladies, Green Ladies, horsemen of various dates, ghosts in armour and even a dreadful old hag. There is also a man's head that portends death in the Donati family of Venice. Inanimate family ghosts are many and varied: blood-red lights; candle lights; drumming sounds; phantom coaches; the sound of crashing crockery; tapping noises; screams and shadows; ghostly harp music (this from Finland); and a dark mist and ghostly coughing (both from America).

POLTERGEISTS

These are probably the most unpleasant of all spontaneous psychic phenomena. Some researchers feel they suggest that on the 'other side' there are malevolent entities who seem to delight in persecuting innocent people; others put the apparently pointless phenomena in the same category as dream activity, manifestations of the unconscious mind – and often the unconscious mind of a disturbed and immature individual.

Other researchers into these difficult fields have suggested that the disturbances (sounds, movement of objects, fire or water appearing from nowhere, etc.) may be 'elementals' – undeveloped or imperfect spirits who play impish (but rarely harmful) tricks and practical jokes like moving things around, overturning objects and spilling the contents, throwing articles. Several observers of so-called poltergeist activity think many of the actions are performed out of exasperation or

A SEVENTEENTH-CENTURY engraving depicting the famous 'Demon Drummer of Tedworth' producing his poltergeistic effects over the house of magistrate John Mompesson; disturbances there lasted about a year and were witnessed by many people including Dr Joseph Glanvill, who was a distinguished divine and philosopher, a Fellow of the Royal Society and a chaplain to Charles II

31

in desperation, as though there is a desire to convey some message but its meaning is never understood.

Many researchers have noticed that poltergeist activity centres around one person in the household, who is often an adolescent but sometimes an elderly person, and when this 'nexus' has been located and is taken to a different environment, the disturbances happen there – the case of a haunted person rather than a haunted house. There is also little that anyone can do about it: poltergeist activity may occur for a few hours, a few days, even a few weeks or months, but then it will cease as mysteriously as it began and nothing anyone does in the meantime makes any difference. Perhaps it is a curious exhibition of an adolescent or immature or frustrated mind finding release in this way.

Mind *can* act upon matter. Our thoughts, conscious and unconscious, can cause reactions upon or within our bodies. In one scientific experiment a researcher held the blunt end of a pencil against the back of a suggestible subject and told her it was a lighted cigarette. Unconsciously the mind of the subject reacted to the idea that it was indeed a lighted cigarette that had touched her back and a 'burn'

POLTERGEIST PHENOMENA were experienced in this house in Hätzingen, Switzerland. Apparitions were seen and objects appeared to fly around; voices, knocking and chains rattling were heard

resulted. This being so it does not seem to be too far-fetched to suggest that at least some 'poltergeist' phenomena may be the result of concentration and mind over matter. A well-known dowser – someone who searches for water with a divining rod – visiting my home on one occasion admired my wife's collection of blue-and-white china displayed on a dresser and said he thought it rather dangerous for anyone with powers of concentration could cause a plate to fall – and most certainly he could, if required.

Poltergeist 'activity' occurs in all parts of the world and has been reported for centuries. The incidents are sometimes surprisingly similar, often beginning with stone-throwing, which was extremely widely reported in primitive societies. One person in the household usually appeared to be at the centre of the disturbances and this person was frequently an adolescent, either a boy or a girl but more commonly a girl. In a number of cases this young person would be maladjusted and sometimes they had physical abnormalities. Because the youngster often resorted to trickery – out of frustration when 'real' activity did not occur in the presence of witnesses – the 'poltergeist activity' was suspected to be an outlet for thwarted instincts. One investigator has also noted that the skill with which the child produces the 'phenomena' after a few weeks' practice, is often quite extraordinary.

In the case of elderly people, often lonely, unhappy and frustrated men or women, who complain of being poked, touched or slapped by the persecuting poltergeist, the 'phenomenon' is sometimes found to be attributable to neurotic delusions or, in some cases, tactile hallucinations. In other cases where there are reported knockings, tappings, thumpings, rumblings and hissing

FASQUE, FETTERCAIRN, in Scotland, where every room seems to be haunted – not always by anything visible but by things sensed, heard and felt. Mr Peter Gladstone, the present owner, says: 'It is an insensitive person who does not meet spirits at Fasque – it's the most haunted house I know.'

THE HAUNTED house at Amherst, Nova Scotia, USA, scene of 'the great Amherst mystery' which lasted exactly a year. Ghostly activity included threats to kill written on walls, movement of objects, inexplicable fires and sounds like thunder claps. This classic case of haunting was written up by a contemporary witness

noises, the origin may be a complaint called *tinnitis*, hallucinatory noises caused by inflammation of the middle ear, such noises appearing to the percipient to reach them from outside sources.

A common assertion is that poltergeist activity is usually due to deliberate trickery, but in a carefully-conducted survey that summarized 318 poltergeist cases only 22 were found to be undoubtedly fraudulent and 18 of the others were doubtful or inconclusive. Assuming that all the doubtful cases were fraudulent (which is unlikely) that gives a total of 40, against the unexplained cases totalling 278. If all poltergeist cases were due to trickery or credulity one might expect to find them in greater numbers in developing countries, but examination has shown that the reverse is actually true. England, France, Italy, Germany and the United States have more cases than places such as Haiti, Chile, Barbados and Transylvania. Though this might be explained by more efficient means of communication in civilized countries an impartial survey of the historic evidence provides a good prima-facie case for the existence of such phenomena.

MODERN GHOSTS

These are ghosts of the very recently dead and are frequent and well-authenticated. Ghosts are not always respecters of time and place, any more than they are of people, and we are all more likely to see the ghost of a recently dead person than any other type of ghost, though in all probability we shall not realize that it is a ghost until it has disappeared.

There is a mass of evidence for people seeing modern ghosts in familiar surroundings. Typical is the man who regularly passed a neighbour taking his dog for a walk. One evening he saw the neighbour as usual but without the dog. When he passed some remark the man walked by as though he were not there. When he arrived home he mentioned the incident to his wife, who looked at him aghast: that neighbour had died the night before! On another occasion I investigated a haunted house where the ghost of a young man had been repeatedly reported by several members of the family occupying the house. We eventually discovered that a young man, answering the description of each witness, had recently committed suicide in the house – and indeed in the room where the ghost was most frequently seen.

In 1981 a young married man saw the ghost of his wife less than a week after she had committed suicide. On a sudden impulse she had thrown herself to her death from high up in a tower block. After the trauma of identifying his wife's body the distraught man had gone back to his empty home – to see his wife, smartly dressed and perfumed, waiting to welcome him home as usual. He felt she wanted to apologize for what she had done. Then he learned that a neighbour had seen his dead wife, apparently fit and well, the day after she had committed suicide. After a few days the dead woman was not seen again, so perhaps this Modern Ghost has an affinity with the Crisis Apparition.

CRISIS APPARITIONS

These are ghosts of limited duration and they are rarely, if ever, seen for more than four days, but they are very common and thousands of examples were reported during both World Wars. In peacetime, too, they are one of the commonest spontaneous manifestations and are most often seen by those near and dear to the recently dead person. A good example is recounted from Rhuddlan, North Wales, where a stranger is the percipient.

A retired resident of this quaint old village, once a seaport, received a letter from a former work colleague asking about the area as a place to retire to and he replied at once saying he loved the place. The next day his wife travelled to nearby Rhyl to see her dentist. On her return she noticed a man crossing the road ahead of her and walking in the direction of her house. She took more notice of the stranger when he turned up her path and when he went towards the front window and waved a letter, as though attracting the attention of her husband inside; and then he disappeared round towards the back of the house. She had a really good view of the man: a stocky figure wearing horn-rimmed spectacles, a fawn raincoat and a brown trilby hat. He had a fat, jolly face.

Suspecting it must be someone her husband knew she went in through the front door and was astonished when her husband didn't know what she was talking about; he had seen no man, no one had called at the house, and he didn't know anyone answering her description. Shortly afterwards the husband received a letter in reply to his, informing him that his former colleague had died suddenly. The whole affair was completely forgotten for several years until one day, while sorting through some old photographs, the wife came across one taken at her husband's retirement party and among the colleagues depicted she recognized, without a shadow of a doubt, the stranger she had seen and who had died so soon after writing to her husband.

GHOSTS OF THE LIVING

On occasions people *are* seen after they have been pronounced dead and perhaps 'something' is released at death that lingers, for one reason or another, around the place of death or where the dead person had strong ties or was emotionally involved. But ghosts of *living* people? How can that be? These present a real problem for the psychic researcher. It does seem that certain people, under certain conditions not yet established, are indeed seen in one place when they are indisputably in another place altogether. Nor is this a recently-reported phenomenon. There is a classic case involving a French woman, Emilie Sagée, documented and examined by reputable investigators in the late nineteenth century.

As a young school-teacher she lost several positions because of her unconscious faculty for being seen in two places at the same time. She would be seen by fellow teachers in the grounds of the school and seconds afterwards they would see her teaching a class, where she had been for over an hour. Another time she was seen in the grounds from the window of a classroom where she was teaching; and on yet another occasion pupils were upset and frightened to see *two* Madame Sagées, side by side at the blackboard! In the end she left teaching and was lost to paranormal investigation.

I even played a personal part in an experience of this type. During the latter years that I worked in publishing in London I was in the habit of popping out for coffee most mornings to a nearby coffee house. Naturally I became known to the proprietor, who would give me a nod as I walked to my usual seat and then bring me a cup of black coffee. One morning my friend James Turner called to see me at the office and we walked round the corner for a cup of coffee. The proprietor looked hard at me for a moment as we walked in and then asked me whether I had been in already that morning. I said 'No, of course not, why?' He said a little earlier he had seen me come in and go through to my usual seat, and he had followed a moment later with my coffee – but when he looked I was not anywhere in the coffee house. He said I had been wearing a different suit to the one I was now wearing but he was absolutely certain it had been me. There was no way in or out of the establishment other than past the proprietor.

Ghostly Inanimate Objects and Animal Ghosts

Equally puzzling to the ghost-equals-spirit enthusiast is the overwhelming evidence for ghostly inanimate objects and animal ghosts. The former, ranging from clocks and chairs to cars, aeroplanes and trains, have been reliably reported for centuries.

Armchairs are one of the commonest articles of haunted furniture and I have come across a dozen or so in the last few years. Sometimes it is a particular figure that is seen and even photographed in the chair, sometimes it is movement of the chair without anyone touching it, sometimes there is evidence that unexplained things happen in the vicinity of the chair, no matter how many times it may be moved.

THE RUINS of Gurre Castle, north of Copenhagen in Denmark, are said to be haunted by a hunt and a ghostly boat

A FAMOUS haunted chair was to be seen for years at the Busby Stoop Inn, Sandhutton, Yorkshire. There were stories that anyone occupying the chair, reserved for the ghost of a hanged murderer, would die within a few weeks

Hans Holzer, the American parapsychologist, has related the story of Bernard and John Simon of New York. The brothers bought a rather strange throne-like chair which they were told was of Mexican-Indian origin. A few days after they had taken it home, Bernard Simon found himself suddenly wide awake in the middle of the night. There was more than enough light in the bedroom to distinguish objects, and his eyes were drawn to the recently-acquired chair. In the chair sat a man. His back was to the bed but it was clear to Bernard that the man was exceptionally tall. Before he could challenge the intruder, or even call out, the figure had completely disappeared.

Holzer took part in a seance at which an entity calling itself Huaska claimed that he recognized Bernard Simon as his reincarnated son. He claimed to have influenced the brothers to purchase the chair, which had once been his, and having done so he was anxious to make himself known and seen. This having been accomplished he was satisfied, and the Indian indicated that he would not trouble the brothers further. For the following few days a number of knocks and other sounds were noticed in the vicinity of the chair, but then all was quiet and the figure of the Indian was seen no more. One is inclined to wonder what might happen if the chair were sold or passed into other hands.

MISS SYBIL *Corbet photographed the interior of Combermere Abbey, Cheshire, England, in 1891. When her photograph of the library was developed it showed the figure of a man sitting in an armchair. The figure seems not to have any legs, but was recognized as that of Lord Combermere – who had been in the habit of using that particular chair. But at the time the photograph was taken his body was being buried some four miles away*

THE OLD aerodrome at Montrose in Scotland, where there are two well-authenticated ghosts: a pilot from an aircraft that crashed here in 1913; and an officer in the Second World War who also died in a plane crash here. Both figures have been seen on numerous occasions by reliable witnesses

A phantom train reportedly appeared each April for several consecutive years on the New York Central Railway at Albany, New York. It was President Abraham Lincoln's funeral train of 27 April 1865 retracing its slow and melancholy journey from Washington to Illinois. According to local and national reports, including the *Albany Evening Times*, hundreds of railway workers made a point of waiting alongside the track in the early evening of each 27 April, waiting for the ghost train.

Another ghost train, its lights blazing, has been reported on the Tay Bridge in Scotland at midnight on 28 December, the anniversary of the Tay Bridge railway disaster of 1879. Part of the bridge which had been opened in 1878, together with a train passing over it, was blown into the river below.

The ghost of a First World War aircraft and its pilot has long been reported from the old Montrose airfield in Scotland, where Sir Peter Masefield, a former Director-General of England's Ministry of Civil Aviation, saw the ghost 'plane in 1963. There are reports of ghost cars in Scotland and Australia; ghost ships off South Africa and the East Coast of America; a haunted oak tree in France; a ghostly motorcyclist in Canada; a haunted doll in Connecticut; a haunted bible in Norfolk, Virginia; a haunted rocking chair in a cheerful yellow cottage on Nantucket Island; even whole buildings and scenes which have no reality; while haunted pictures are legion everywhere. And, of course, there are ghost horses, dogs, cats and other animals by the score and in many countries.

SANDFORD ORCAS Manor House in Dorset, England, has long been haunted by several ghosts, including a butler, a man in a white smock, a woman in red, a terrier dog, a woman in Elizabethan dress and a harpsichord player. 'Beautiful music' has been heard in the room over the gatehouse

A GHOSTLY white rabbit gambols about the churchyard of the ancient church at Egloshayle, in Cornwall, England. Those who have attempted to trap it or attack it have found that the 'animal' has suddenly vanished. No one knows the history of the ghost rabbit, but it has been reported for generations

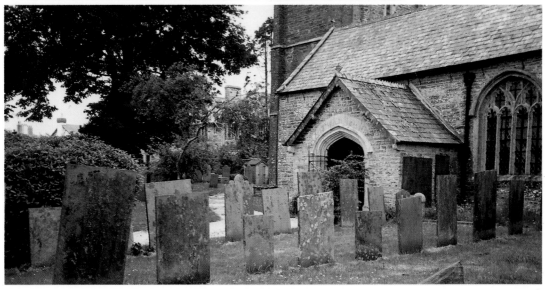

A classic story of a ghost dog dates back to the American Civil War, when a Confederate spy was captured with his dog and sentenced to be shot. He asked for his dog for company during his last night on earth, but this request was refused and the dog was taken away and slaughtered. Next morning, as he faced the firing squad, he saw his dog approaching and he greeted it. The firing squad saw nothing and thought he was mad, so he was hastily blindfolded. But Colonel Panton, who was in charge of the execution, went deathly pale and apparently *did* see the ghost dog. Three times he tried to give the order to fire, but no words came and at length, visibly shaken, he muttered 'Execution deferred' and dismissed the squad. That night the Confederates attacked, Colonel Panton was killed, the condemned soldier was released and he then learned that his dog had been killed the previous day. To the end of his life he maintained that his dead pet had returned to save his life.

While many parapsychologists would argue that spontaneous ghostly activity falls into some of the categories in this chapter, there also seem to be Mixed Hauntings, which contain attributes of several different types – and even additional elements – so it can be very difficult to 'spot the difference' as far as ghosts are concerned.

Those I have detailed ignore several other categories that well repay investigation. Years ago, for instance, I carried out extensive

THE BULL Hotel, Long Melford, England. Scene of a murder in the seventeenth century, many mysterious happenings have been reported here over the years

INNS AND hotels are often haunted and the Dolphin Hotel in Penzance, Cornwall, has been home over the years to several ghosts and much ghostly activity

investigations which established that there are more haunted rectories, parsonages and such-like than any other types of inhabited building, and more haunted churches than any other type of uninhabited building. Could it be that concentrated thought (common to both these categories) can have something to do with the production of ghosts? There are also many haunted ruins and prehistoric sites; many haunted theatres and inns and hotels – although the latter must always be suspect in view of today's fascination with ghosts and ghostly happenings.

It is never easy to decide exactly which ghost you are dealing with (*if* it is a genuine ghost) but to do so is essential so that you can deal with it in an appropriate manner.

Ghosts

THE EVIDENCE WORLDWIDE

Stone Age man buried his dead with ceremonies that he believed would ensure that they rested easily in an after life. The ancient Semitic people of Babylonia were convinced that the dead visited the earth in spirit form. The Assyrians defined ghosts as difficult, evil spirits who could cause illness or presage a death; restless gibbering spirits; friendly apparitions; and ghosts that returned temporarily for a single purpose, usually to right some wrong.

The ancient Egyptians believed they could communicate with the dead and that they could ease the journey after death by embalmment and the supply of various articles, and food and drink, which were buried with their dead. Executed criminals, those drowned at sea and the unburied dead were especially likely to return.

The ancient Greeks and Romans provided detailed descriptions of various ghosts including wandering ghosts that could harm the living; ghosts of the virtuous who could influence the living for good; purposeful ghosts and so on. India has always had fearsome ghosts; the Chinese and Japanese ghosts appear in innumerable strange guises –

OPPOSITE: BRAN CASTLE in Rumania, commonly known as Dracula's Castle and reputedly haunted for centuries

KRONBORG CASTLE, in Elsinore, Denmark, inspired Shakespeare's play Hamlet. *Eerie screams have been heard coming from a tower, and a ghostly man dressed in red haunts one of the bastions*

sometimes even changing form; the North American Indians always revered the spirits of the dead and even had their own Ghost Dance. It originated with the son of a Sioux chief who had a vision of going to heaven and seeing God and all the Sioux people who had died. He felt he had been told to return to earth and instruct his people in the Ghost Dance, which would ensure victory and cause the white men to vanish from the earth. The dance was performed with apparent success on several occasions and then just before the skirmish at Wounded Knee, where it proved ineffective. There, for all practical purposes, the Ghost Dance ended. Through all the ages ghosts have been accepted by man, including, of course, in biblical times, and to this day all orthodox religions have services of exorcism which attempt to deal with harmful ghosts. In my experience all exorcisms have a considerable effect on the human occupants of a 'haunted' house but no effect on genuine ghostly activity.

THE MERRY Maidens in Cornwall, where ghostly figures have been seen, is one of scores of ancient stone circles that seem to possess a force or power, almost as though the stones are charged with energy. There is a theory that ghosts and ghostly happenings may be recorded events preserved in the stones and structure of a place

SINCE TIME immemorial a hill near Mold in Wales, known as Goblins Hill, has been said to be haunted by a golden mounted figure that emerges from the hill and shines like a sun. During excavation in the nineteenth-century, a gold peytrel (breastplate for a horse) was unearthed and is now preserved in the British Museum in London. It dates from about 1300 BC and the hill was probably the burial place of an ancient chief, kept alive in folk memory and by his ghostly reappearances

THE HAUNTED catacombs of Rome, where the dust of six million early Christians is entombed, have long been the subject of stories of mysterious happenings – odd sounds, movement of objects, spectres, voices and even the complete disappearance of people. It is certainly all too easy to lose one's way here – in more ways than one

When I compiled the first *Gazetteer of British Ghosts* in 1971 (a dozen such indexes have appeared since) I asserted that 'there are more ghosts seen, reported and accepted in the British Isles than anywhere else on earth'. Seeking to explain the reason why this should be I suggested that 'a unique ancestry with Mediterranean, Scandinavian, Celtic and other strains, an intrinsic island detachment, and enquiring nature, and perhaps our readiness to accept a supernormal explanation for curious happenings may all have played their part in bringing about this state of affairs'.

Other writers offer other observations: 'time-slips' (visions between two periods of actual time) are far more common in the British Isles than anywhere else, they say (but why?); as are 'recordings' of past events being replayed according to a set of natural circumstances – possibly the result of a combination of atmospheric, geological and mental components – but why could this not happen anywhere where there was a similar combination?

It may well be that there *are* more reported ghosts per square mile in the British Isles than anywhere else on earth, although there are hundreds of dramatic and well-authenticated accounts of ghostly activity in many parts of the world, and there is undoubtedly some ghostly activity that we never hear about.

WESTEINDE 12, THE HAGUE

First-hand evidence for the haunting of the former British Embassy in The Hague in Holland was supplied to me by Sir Peter Garron, a former British Ambassador to Holland. The story of the house on the Westeinde, a street in that city, begins over five hundred years ago when the house was a hunting lodge of the counts of Holland. In the middle of the fifteenth century a man of substance, Garrit van Assendelft, lived at what was then known as the House of Assendelft. His grandson Ridder Garrit van Assendelft, went to France to study law in Orleans. There he met and married a girl named Catherine de Chasseur, who is regarded as the source of the ghostly happenings that have since been reported.

The marriage was disastrous. Ridder tried to leave his wife behind when he returned home but she followed him to The Hague and, when he refused to admit her to his house, the Court ordered him to take her 'to live with him in his house, at his table and in his bed'. But it was no good, and the marriage broke up in 1532.

After the legal separation Catherine left the house with their child, Nicholaes or Claes, while Ridder (now known by his patronymic as Garrit) prospered and became a man of considerable importance and influence. He was a favourite of the Emperor, Charles V, and from 1528 until 1558 was President of the Court. Catherine, for her part, is said to have lived up to the rank of her husband and was extravagant. To make ends meet she seems to have taken to counterfeiting money. On 11 February 1541, she was caught red-handed with her accomplices and at her trial she was condemned to be burned to death at the stake in public. But her sentence was commuted to private execution and, on 11 April 1541 in the Genvengepoort Prison she suffered the gruesome water death, being filled with water until she expired. Her accomplices were beheaded.

In about 1754 the Spanish Ambassador of the day had the old house pulled down and he built the existing residence. It changed hands a number of times and in the nineteenth century it was presented to the Jesuit fathers, who own it to this day. The British Minister at The Hague in 1861, Sir Andrew Buchanan, took a lease on the house and this lease was renewed again and again.

There have been persistent rumours over many years about the existence of a ghost in the house, and Sir Horace Rumbold, who was Minister from 1888 to 1896, refers to these disturbances in his memoirs. He mentions one particular upstairs room as being haunted, where the occupants were plagued by vivid nightmares, 'though the recurrence in them of the same distinctive features, were singularly akin to spectral visitations'. His successor gave up using the room as a bedroom and turned it into a boxroom. Certainly, says Sir Horace, 'we were all of us from the first conscious of an indefinable atmosphere of creepiness and mystery pervading the entire rambling building after dark'. He goes on to say that it was only towards the end of his tenancy that he became aware of the unhappy story of the French girl, Catherine de Chasseur.

The first known reference to a ghost in the house is in a letter to a Johan de Witt from his sister, Johanna. On 16 August 1653 she wrote telling her brother that a maid she had engaged was unwilling to sleep alone in the house because she had heard that it was haunted.

There is a reference to the ghost, too, in a book by Meriel Buchanan, daughter of Sir George Buchanan, Minister from 1908 to 1910. She says that two maids left in succession complaining that someone, or something, 'had tried to pull the covers off their beds in the middle of the night', and she goes on to say that she herself had once experienced the same sensation. She had immediately put on a light but found no one in the room, although she did hear the rustle of a dress, 'as if someone had hurriedly left the room'.

In the records of the haunting there are a number of references to 'watery manifestations' (which could perhaps be significant in view of the manner of Catherine de Chasseur's death); and during the occupation of Sir Odo Russell, Minister from 1928 to 1933, there were many reports of poltergeist-like activity: doors opening unaccountably; articles removed from drawers and scattered about rooms; water lying about in unexpected places; and taps found inexplicably turned on. The Russell children had no doubt whatever about an unseen presence in the small room at the end of an upstairs passage (perhaps the same room that had provoked 'nightmares'), then known as 'the train room' because the youngest boy, David, had his train set laid out there. One day David, alone in the room, was quite certain that the 'presence' was between him and the door and although he finally managed to escape, he never wanted to play trains in that room again.

The most remarkable manifestation of all occurred one evening at this period in the dining-room, where the table was laid out for a large dinner party. Suddenly, just before eight o'clock, water poured from the ceiling, falling exactly in the place where the hostess was to sit! The table was hurriedly moved to the ballroom and reset, but the strange thing was that afterwards there was no sign of water damage to the ceiling.

There are also reports of a ghostly lady with her head covered, walking along the upstairs passage during the time of Sir Paul Mason (1954-60), and of the Masons' dog, an inveterate barker, suddenly crouching back in the same passage, all its hackles up, absolutely quiet but obviously very frightened. At the same time an English girl then living at the house heard unexplained footsteps and saw the handle of the door to the 'haunted bedroom' slowly turn. The door was in fact locked, but there was no sound of the footsteps retreating from it; and when the girl had sufficiently recovered herself to unlock the door, she found nothing inside to explain what she had heard and seen.

Sir Peter Garron told me that he felt that although these two 'manifestations' might possibly be discounted, 'other occurrences are

THE HAUNTED cellars of the former British Embassy at The Hague – Weistende 12, where there have been reports of curious happenings over the years

less easily explicable'. When I asked Sir Peter whether he, or his family, had seen the ghost lady he did not find the question easy to answer. He told me that one evening, after a Jesuit priest had been to tea, he and his wife were sitting at dinner. Something shadowy seemed to pass between them and he saw what looked like a waving line of smoke or the misty outline of a full and flowing dress moving slowly across the table. His wife did not notice anything and Sir Peter said he could offer no logical explanation for his experience. Brinkman, the Garrons' butler, who had been at the Embassy for over forty years, certainly believed he saw the ghost. When asked to describe it, and knowing nothing of Sir Peter's experience, Brinkman said he had seen 'a shadowy figure with a grey and smoky skirt'. The haunting of Westeinde 12 is an enthralling story and an historical haunting that may well continue.

SOME AMERICAN GHOSTS

The curious Winchester Mystery House in San José, California, might be described as a monument to death. Sarah Winchester, one of the most remarkable women in the history of the American West, spent nearly forty years here alone in a house she never stopped enlarging. The story goes that Sarah, who died quietly in her sleep (as far as is known) in 1922, believed that the spirits of all those killed by Winchester rifles had placed a curse on her, the last of the line, but that she might escape the curse by building a house, and as long as the building work continued she would avert ghostly vengeance.

THE LABYRINTHINE structure of the Winchester Mystery House in San José, California, with its unfinished rooms, secret staircases and doors that lead nowhere (see above)

The unhappy widow and mother, whose only child had died within a fortnight of being born, purchased an eight-room farmhouse and then proceeded to rebuild and extend it, work that continued every day for the remaining thirty-eight years of her life, including Sundays and national holidays. She communed with the spirits each night and, in accordance with their wishes, she claimed, she built or added room after room, balcony after balcony, window after window, chimney after chimney, stairway after stairway, until there were upwards of 160 rooms connected by miles of twisting and winding corridors, indoor and outdoor balconies, steep and shallow stairways; not to mention the scores of trick doors, interconnecting or dead-end balconies, passageways and stairways. The whole baffling labyrinth was devised by ghosts for ghosts, if we are to believe Sarah Winchester. Certainly, since her death ghostly happenings have been repeatedly rumoured: footsteps; whispering; the sound of rattling chains; cold spots; icy draughts; balls of red light; and phantom forms. All these and more have been reported within the last couple of years.

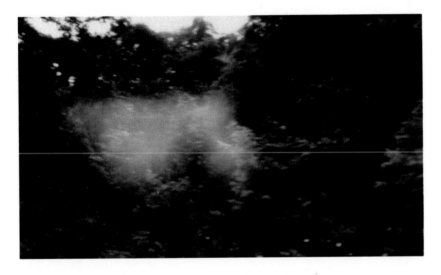

A MYSTERIOUS mist was witnessed and photographed, in Bachelor's Grove cemetery in Chicago, Illinois. There have been reports of haunting there over the years

Room 502 at the Hotel del Coronado, Orange Avenue, Coronado, San Diego, California, is one hotel room where you might encounter ghostly activity. Certainly the room, reputedly the scene of a suicide many years ago, has been haunted for decades, through five successive owners. The room is normally only available when all other accommodation is filled, so if you care to take the risk, ask especially for Room 502. This grand hotel was the setting for the Marilyn Monroe film *Some Like It Hot* (1958) and has been patronized by eight United States presidents. It was here, at a special occasion held in his honour in 1920, that the then Prince of Wales met and danced with his future duchess, Wallace Simpson.

Mrs Betty Shields had lived in the same house in Sewickley,

Pennsylvania, built between 1849 and 1854, for forty years but still found it a sad and melancholy place. 'I don't think the spirits like you coming here', she said, as we entered the old mansion. The snow swirled in through the open door and the wind rattled at the casements. She explained that a sash-cord had broken and that the window had dropped open with a frightening clatter just a few minutes before our arrival. 'I think the old house still remembers the day young William Chaplin Shields rode off to war. He never came back and they never found his body. The family, and particularly his father, never got over the tragedy.'

Mrs Shields, a slight grey-haired woman of middle years, had been the editor of the village paper until her retirement and has a feel for history. She was proud to tell the story of Captain William Shields and his hero's death in the American Civil War. William was last seen, sabre drawn, leading a charge at the battle of Chancellorsville, in early May, 1863. His men said later that he was cut down by withering Confederate fire. His remains were never recovered when the battle was over, but some say his spirit returned to the old house in Sewickley.

The pretty Pennsylvanian village on the banks of the mighty Ohio River was home to the company of men who had ridden off with young William during those heady, euphoric days in 1861 when war was declared. They eventually became part of the Army of the Potomac, fighting for the Union cause. Many did not return but are still remembered to this day. Some are buried in the cemetery above the village. Others found their resting place in the military cemetery at Gettysburg.

'No one knows where William came to rest', said Mrs Shields. 'Some believe his spirit haunts this house even now. For years after the conflict, his father would walk the floors, hour after hour. The younger brother, David, also went to war and was twice wounded. But William was the favourite. He was a most handsome man – fair-haired and with a military bearing.'

The old family eventually passed away – the father before the turn of the new century and the surviving brother as an old man in the 1940s. The stories told by the veterans were almost forgotten and younger family members inherited the property.

Leet Shields was a bomber pilot in the Second World War and married Betty, a girl from a nearby town, on his return from Europe. They settled in the house and brought up a son. William and David were always remembered on Veterans Day in late May, and visitors would often ask about the portrait over the fireplace in the living-room. William had never sat for the portrait, but a local artist had painstakingly copied it from an old sepia print taken before he set out for war. They said the likeness was excellent. The dark blue uniform now looks rather dull with age, but the eyes are clear and the features clean cut and strong.

The room still looks as it would have done a century ago. Fine furniture is well positioned along each wall and surrounds the comfortable armchairs, which give a hint of a more relaxed, slower-moving age. Only the carpet, in a dusty pink which blends well with the deep mahogany, gives a hint of modern times.

It was in this setting that a strange and frightening incident occurred a few years ago. It was summer and the Shields were entertaining friends from England. Jean and David were keen to see the old mansion – it was one of the few ante-bellum properties remaining in Allegheny County and had changed little over the years. The long and airy hallway, always cool and dark even on a stifling summer's day, dominated the ground floor of the house. Reception rooms led off on each side of this corridor and the living-room, with the painting of William, was first on the right. But guests were always entertained to cocktails on the wide, south-facing veranda. It was cool there, out of the sun, and the lawn and trees, which fell away to the roadway, were an attractive backdrop to the conversation.

THE SHIELDS mansion, which has changed little since it was built in 1854. The windows of the haunted room are on the right of the veranda

The party went in for lunch at about noon and only Jean and Mrs Shields remained on the porch. They were engaged in conversation for the better part of ten minutes and then turned to follow the party. Mrs Shields went first and Jean followed. The latter entered the hall but, in the gloom, opened the wrong door. In an instant she realized her mistake, but it was too late. In front of her were five strange figures she had not expected to see. She stood frozen in her tracks. They turned and she gasped with shock!

One standing figure was in the dark-blue uniform of the Union army. By his side was a tall woman, her hair dressed in the severe, unflattering style of the mid-nineteenth century. Seated on the sofa were three other women engaged in deep conversation with their male companion. All were dressed in the crinolines of the day and wearing the neat, lace caps which Victorian ladies chose for indoors.

They all turned to look at Jean. Nobody spoke but the mood was unfriendly. They gazed at her as if she were an intruder, eavesdropping on their conversation. Terrified, she fled from the room, calling out for her husband. The plea in her voice brought other members of the party hurrying from the dining-room, where lunch was being served. Now speechless, she pointed to the heavy living-room door which had slammed behind her. David threw it open, only to be confronted by an empty sofa and undisturbed chairs. The room was empty!

The visit took on a more sombre note after the incident in the living-room. The conversation turned to past members of the family and their heroic deeds of long ago. Had Jean burst in on a meeting of William Chaplin Shields and his four sisters? We will never know. Her descriptions fitted those people long since gone.

Mrs Betty Shields is convinced William comes back to the house. 'He has nowhere to rest and this was his home', she told me.

THIS OLD bridge at Richmond in Tasmania was built by convict labour and is haunted by a man who walks across it and by a brutal overseer who was thrown into the river by the men

ANOTHER AUSTRALIAN ghost was photographed by the Rev. R S Blance at Corroboree Rock, 100 miles from Alice Springs, in 1959. This is an old aborigine initiation ceremony site, and no one else was in the area when the photograph was taken

FISHER'S GHOST, AUSTRALIA

Alasdair Alpin MacGregor, an eminent English civil servant and member of the Ghost Club, first told me about Fisher's Ghost. During his travels in Australia MacGregor used the main road south from Sydney to Melbourne. Not far from Cambelltown he saw a signboard: 'Fisher's Ghost Creek'. Making enquiries he learned a curious story from a local doctor who had been interested in the matter for several years.

Fisher was the name of a man who had been murdered but whose body had never been found. There were a number of reports of Fisher's ghost being seen sitting in a particular position on a bridge and pointing, and between them the doctor and MacGregor, after some research, succeeded in plotting the exact spot where the ghost had been seen. Digging was carried out and Fisher's body was found.

Eventually the murderer was discovered and in due course he was hanged, so justice seems to have been carried out through the appearance of a ghost. After the discovery of the body there were no more reports of the ghost of Fisher appearing at the scene of the crime.

ORIENTAL GHOSTS

Ghosts in the Orient are usually taken for granted and many people thoroughly accept ghosts. A town in Japan even has an annual holiday for entertaining visitors from the other world – the Feast of Lanterns – each September.

To the Chinese, too, the dead are never far away although they are not always welcome. A large house in Peking stood empty for years because of its haunted reputation until a man from Shanghai, unaware of the stories of ghosts, bought a lease on the property and moved in with his wife. After they had been there only a few days he was called away on business, and when he returned he found his wife living in the gatehouse, afraid to go back into the main house.

Each night as she was about to retire, she told her husband, the ghostly form of a young lady appeared in a corner of the room. First a hand would appear, then an ornate head-dress, then the head, face and body. When the figure began to moan softly the frightened wife would flee to the gatehouse. The husband, thinking the neighbours must be playing tricks, decided to be ready for them. That night as he and his wife went to bed in their bedroom in the big house, he waited in the next room, armed with a sword.

After a while he heard a slight hissing sound and what appeared to be the form of a young woman began to take shape in the corner of the room. The man ran in and attacked the figure with his sword, whereupon it vanished, but left behind an ornate Manchu head-dress.

The husband took the head-dress to the police and told them his story. He also went to see his landlord and said he wanted to cancel the lease and move out of the house. The landlord agreed, but asked to be shown exactly where the ghost had appeared. He then engaged workmen, who broke down the wall and floor beneath and dug into the foundation. At length the remains of an old coffin were found and in it a corpse dressed in Manchu costume. Part of the head-dress was missing.

It seemed that the house had once been owned by a Manchu family, members of whom were traced. They revealed that some two centuries earlier martial law had been declared in the area and the city gates were closed for a time. Even the dead had to be buried in improvised graves and when a young woman had died she had been buried in a corner of the courtyard. A house had later been built over the grave and the coffin had been crushed by the foundations.

The Chinese believe that everyone has a 'grave soul' attached to the body and staying with it in death; in this case the 'grave soul' had come back to reveal its fate to successive occupants of the house over the grave. The landlord had the corpse removed, placed in another coffin and buried in the family graveyard and there was no more trouble in the house.

The famous Raffles Hotel in Singapore has long been reputed to be ghost-ridden and in 1985 one witness told me that the back wing, off Buser Road, is haunted by a disembodied voice, sounding very much like a schoolgirl, singing an English nursery rhyme. Apparently this psychic echo has been heard by hundreds of visitors (who have no previous knowledge of the mysterious and ghostly voice) and by the staff and permanent occupants of the hotel. Interestingly enough the hotel occupies a site where once there stood a boarding school for English girls, so this ghost probably dates back to before 1897.

GHOSTS IN INDIA

India is renowned for a number of memorable ghost stories. There is the remarkable Poona poltergeist – a tale that involved a famous Indian historian and his cultured German wife, an English medical man who was called in to give his professional advice. It was a case that completely satisfied Father Herbert Thurston SJ, a Roman Catholic priest with a lifelong interest in psychical manifestation. The case lasted for many years and disturbances included: interference with bedclothes; movement of objects – including articles hurled with considerable force around corners; the appearance and disappearance of objects, etc.; all usually in the vicinity of a lad of eight years old, and sometimes observed in broad daylight. The evidence of various impeccable and responsible witnesses satisfied the critical Thurston.

There is also the well-documented Pillay case that lasted just sixteen days: clothes, holy pictures and other articles inexplicably burst into flames; chalk crosses were rubbed out; objects disappeared; tin plates were rolled up; vessels containing milk were spilled in puzzling circumstances; cooking utensils rose unaided to the ceiling and then fell to the ground and broke; bricks and stones were thrown; writings appeared on walls; water sprang from nowhere, and a dark female figure was seen. All these incidents, and others, were detailed at the time of the disturbances by Mr Pillay, a Sub-Magistrate in the Tanjore district.

SOME OTHER POLTERGEISTS

From Russia, with the authority of Ghost Club member A. Aksakoff, State-Counsellor to His Imperial Majesty the Tsar of Russia, comes a poltergeist case that became the subject of an official enquiry. The case included small objects and bricks and stones being thrown about closed rooms; loud knocking sounds; heavy objects being moved; an axe being thrown with considerable force; a bed catching fire; window panes suddenly breaking and the sound of human groaning. All were quite inexplicable in the circumstances related and were witnessed by the local head of police, an Army captain and his wife, and various other people.

From a remote farm in the Province of Quebec, Canada, comes the story of a 35-year-old farmer, his wife and three children being plagued by equally mysterious happenings which, once again, included movement of objects, smashed windows, outbreaks of fire and the appearance of water. Also, a child's braid of hair was cut off; a gruff voice was heard – as of an old man seemingly very near at hand; the figure of a white-haired man was seen, and that of a black dog that had no reality. All this continued for over three months and is verified by upwards of seventeen witnesses, all of whom were responsible people living in the district. Then everything stopped just as mysteriously as it had begun.

ELSEWHERE IN Canada, ghosts and strange happenings have been reported from the Old City Hall in Toronto (photographed in 1914) over the years – by many people, including two judges in 1980

HAUNTED GUERNSEY

Victor Hugo, the nineteenth-century French poet and author, lived in Guernsey, in the Channel Islands. His house at St Peter Port is haunted and is *almost* appropriately named Hauteville House. Hugo's daughter, Adèle, an accomplished pianist, eventually went mad and died in the house. Years later, when there was no piano in there, the sound of exquisite piano playing was heard originating from the room where her piano once stood. A visitor occupying the room above Adèle's former music room heard the sounds quite distinctly on several occasions in 1980 but immediate investigation revealed no explanation. These sounds, always originating from the same room, have been reported by successive curators and this curious psychic disturbance is very well known locally.

Also in Guernsey, an underground bunker, half military hospital and half ammunition store and just part of a huge underground installation built by the Nazis, has long had the reputation of being haunted. Fifty-four slave labourers lie buried nearby, while an unknown number are still embedded where they died in the bunker. Guernsey people don't go there and many of the visitors find the place distinctly disturbing: some people come out in tears; others are very frightened; while some hide their discomfort by giggling nervously. When the bunker was used for a film twenty years ago, inexplicable happenings, accidents and sounds repeatedly interrupted the filming, as Peter Sellers, one of the stars of the film and a Ghost Club member, told me. In fact, he said, he had never been so frightened anywhere in his life.

MORE EUROPEAN GHOSTS

In France there are many haunted châteaux: the Loire Valley has Blois, where Joan of Arc had her standards blessed by the Archbishop of Reims and where two ghosts walk. One is the ghost of a murderer who was himself murdered, and the other is the ghost of his victim.

THE HAUNTED tower of Château Gratot, former manor of the Argouges, near Coutances in Normandy, France. The narrow passages and winding stairs retain some of the tragedy enacted here, and the ghosts of a man and a woman have been seen on countless occasions, frequently in bright sunlight

THE TOWERS of Blois, on the skyline beyond the Gabriel Bridge, in the Loire Valley in France, where two ghosts walk – the ghost of a murderer and his victim

The royal ghost and murderer is Henri III of France, who came to the throne in 1574. He feared the growing popularity of his witty and attractive rival, Henri de Guise, and murdered him in the royal bedroom on the second floor. After the killing Henri went to his mother, Catherine de Medici, and said, 'I no longer have a rival; the so-called King of Paris is dead'. 'God grant', Catherine replied, 'that you have not just become the King of Nothing at All!' Her intuition was prophetic, and a few months later Henri himself was stabbed to death. The unmistakable ghosts of the two 'kings' have been authoritatively reported on many occasions.

One of the most beautiful of the châteaux of the Loire is Chenonceaux. Here Charles IX used to dress his courtiers as mermaids, nymphs and satyrs to welcome and amuse his guests, and one can still admire the beautiful Diane de Poitiers Italian garden and the equally fine Catherine de Medici garden. Both women are reported to haunt this gracious building. Catherine de Medici, wife of Henri II, reappears on nights of the full moon, combing the hair of her rival, Diane de Poitiers, mistress of the King and regarded as the most beautiful woman in France. When Henri died his jealous wife exiled Diane de Poitiers from Chenonceaux, the one place on earth she truly loved and where her ghost is still seen, pale and sad, at the time of the full moon before the great mirror in her bedroom.

In the north of England my wife and I visited Philomena, Lady de Hoghton, at her hauntingly beautiful home Hoghton Tower near Preston in Lancashire. The conversation soon turned to ghosts and we learned of the ghostly lady in green velvet; the loud laughter that has no rational explanation; the unexplained rustling of a heavy silken skirt;

THIS PAINTING by George Cattermole shows James I visiting Hoghton Tower, Lancashire, England, in 1617. One of the best-known ghosts here, the tragic Ann Hoghton, may date from about this period

and the ghost of a daughter of the house, Ann, who, when the Hoghtons were Protestant, fell in love with a Catholic young man who lived nearby at Samlesbury Hall.

They planned to elope, and from her hiding place Ann saw him silently arrive. She sped to greet him, but word of the attempted elopement had reached the ears of her parents and as Ann watched her lover slid off his horse, dead at her feet, killed by her father. Ann never recovered from the shock and she never forgave those who had killed her one true love. Soon she went into a nunnery and she stayed there for the rest of her life. But in thoughts and dreams she must often have gone back to Hoghton Tower and, by all accounts, she returns in ghostly form, from time to time, usually appearing in the banqueting hall.

THE JACK and Jill windmills on Duncton Down in Sussex (from a drawing by F L Bussell)

At Duncton Down, in Sussex, England, there are two windmills, known as Jack and Jill, which have long been reputed to be haunted. Captain Walter Anson, a biographer, and his wife went to live there in 1911 and stayed until Mrs Anson died forty years later. She loved the place and created gardens from the former bleak downland. It is thought to be her ghost that haunts the place.

In 1953 Henry Longhurst, the golfer and writer, bought the Jack and Jill mills and he and his wife had no doubt that Mrs Anson haunted the bungalow. Many times, Longhurst told me, he and his wife heard her characteristic cough (she died of a chest infection). Whether the room in which she died was empty or occupied by guests the inexplicable coughing was still heard. The ghost of Mrs Anson was also thought to be responsible for unexplained bell ringing; movement of objects; and other strange happenings. When the bungalow was developed in 1963 the manifestations ceased as mysteriously as they had begun. (It has been noticed that structural alterations in an allegedly haunted house often either promote phenomena or bring them to a stop.)

There seems to be little or no essential difference between twentieth-century apparitions and those of the eighteenth or nineteenth centuries. The most striking impression left from random samplings of modern and ancient reports is that the appearances are usually pointless and harmless and often unrecognized; but that ghosts are seen, throughout the world, cannot be denied.

Ghosts

Can They be Photographed?

The photography of spontaneous ghosts is a chancy and unreliable business: occasionally a misty, or even a clear, image is obtained of something that cannot be explained logically; but far more frequently nothing registers on the film although something may be visible (or apparently visible) to the human eye.

Incidentally, rather more success has been obtained in recording sounds reportedly made by ghosts: voices; whispering (the words are usually indistinct); cries; footsteps (curiously, the recorded noise of footsteps is often louder than remembered by the witness); door-opening or -closing; the sounds of a dog or a cat; and so on.

There are also frequent reports of phantom smells, usually pleasant and, if floral, often completely out of season, but occasionally most unpleasant; the smell of tobacco or strong drink has also been recorded and other smells, such as food being cooked, but all these, sadly, depend upon human testimony.

IN 1963 the Rev. Kenneth Lord took a photograph of the altar in Newby Church, in Yorkshire, England. He saw nothing unusual through the viewfinder and the church was completely deserted, yet on the resulting photograph a tall, staring, hooded and transparent figure is clearly visible. The photograph has been thoroughly examined by a Home Office laboratory specially equipped for enhancing photographic images. Their conclusion is that even the most rigorous computer analysis cannot provide a similar photographic image, so this could well be a genuine paranormal photograph

A 'MANIFESTATION' photographed in St Peter's Church in Malvern Wells, England, in 1972 at midday after a private communion. The photograph was taken by Gerald Fox, and is described by the Rev. William Y Milne (who sent me the photograph) as depicting 'a radiant figure of transparent colour and brightness', perhaps a vision of Christ in an act of blessing. Other photographs taken at the same time and place show no similar 'fault'

IS IT A FAKE?

Photographs of ghosts may be the most valuable independent evidence yet obtainable, but the malicious production of so-called 'ghost photographs' is notoriously easy and, in some cases, the results are extremely convincing to anyone other than a person experienced in photography and fraud.

In the Ghost Club of Great Britain we have long had as a valued member Dr Vernon Harrison, a former President of the Royal

Photographic Society, who has examined scores of odd photographs. Only rarely is he unable to suggest a probable normal explanation for one, but on occasions even he finds it difficult to dismiss a photograph sent to him for examination – given the circumstances under which the photograph is said to have been taken. This, of course, is all-important, and it is also necessary to establish beyond any doubt that the photographer and his companions (if any) are above suspicion.

Attempts have been made to photograph ghosts since the earliest days of photography. William Mumler, an engraver, was not even interested in ghosts or 'spirit' photographs, but when processing some of his photographs he found faces that should not have been there. Having photographed members of his family he discovered on his plates (so runs the story) the pictures not only of his living family but also of long-dead relatives. He then carried out what may well have been the first controlled experiment into ghost photography, in 1862. News of his involuntary photography of the dead spread like wildfire through the photographic fraternity world-wide and he made history when his prints were upheld as genuine by the US Court of Appeal Judge, John Edmund, in 1863.

THIS PHOTOGRAPH was taken by Gordon Carroll of Northampton, England, in 1964. The church of St Mary the Virgin, Woodford, Northamptonshire, was deserted at the time and the kneeling monk so clearly depicted in the resulting photograph was not visible to the naked eye

*A TYPICAL example of Mrs
Ada Emma Deane's 'spirit
photographs'*

Similar results were obtained in Britain by Frederick Hudson in 1872
and his photographs (often showing a filmy, cloud-like effect) were
authenticated by Dr Alfred Russel Wallace, the noted naturalist and
co-originator of the theory of evolution, who was also a Ghost Club
member. But the process had its critics.

In 1898 Dr W J Russell lectured at the Royal Society in London and
provided evidence from his own experiments that such 'ghost'
photographs could be produced fraudulently. Russell demonstrated to
his audience that zinc, nickel, gum copal and even printers' ink could all
produce similar filmy, ghost-like impressions on photographic plates.
Still the matter was not settled, however, for a number of professional
photographers reported finding 'ghost extras' on their plates which could
not be explained by Russell's demonstrations and findings.

Many of the most puzzling ghost photographs were taken in the
presence of spiritualist mediums and some mediums specialized in this
type of mediumship – William Hope and Mrs Ada Emma Deane in
England, in particular. William Hope from Cheshire, England, was,
perhaps, the most famous or notorious 'spirit photographer' and in his
'Crewe circle' he produced scores of photographs depicting 'extras' on
them. Eventually, a former Chairman of the Ghost Club of Great
Britain, Mr Harry Price, investigated Hope and wrote a devastating
report that was subsequently verified by other investigators. Mrs Ada
Emma Deane produced one of the biggest fakes in the history of
'spirit' photography with her Armistice Day pictures. The ghost-like
faces turned out to be photographs of well-known living sportsmen!

On the other hand, the French psychical researcher Hippolyte
Baraduc took a photograph of his dead son as he lay in his coffin and a
formless mass of broken white cloud or mist showed up on the
resulting print. Baraduc explained the misty mass as the departed soul

of his son. Six months later Baraduc's wife died, and as she breathed her last three gentle sighs her husband photographed the event, and three luminous globes were seen hovering over the body. Another photograph taken shortly afterwards shows the globes combined as one, and this Baraduc believed to be his wife's soul, leaving the body.

The eminent Dr Hereward Carrington, long-time director of the American Psychical Institute, said, after working for fifty years in the field of psychical research, 'Despite the amount of fraud which enters into the subject of so-called spirit photography, I am nevertheless convinced that there are cases of genuine phenomena – in which strange and abnormal markings appear upon photographic negatives when no such markings should be present'. He was, for example, much impressed by the SS *Watertown* case, and took the trouble to look into it in some detail.

ONE OF 'spirit photographer' Billy (William) Hope's typical 'psychic photographs'

The story, as recounted by Carrington and as detailed in the house magazine of the shipping company, told of the tanker, SS *Watertown*, ploughing its way through the Pacific Ocean. Seamen Courtney and Meehan were assigned to clean out a cargo tank. While doing this work they were overcome by gas fumes and died before help could reach them. Following the tradition of the sea their bodies were committed to the ocean.

The following day, just before dusk, the entire ship was in uproar when the heads of the two dead seamen were clearly seen on board ship and, later, in the sea. Thereafter the ghost faces were frequently seen and understandably became the chief topic of conversation in both officers' and seamen's quarters. The 'ghosts' were, apparently, almost daily visitors to the ship and they were usually seen at the spot where the bodies of the two seamen had been put over the side. Then someone suggested taking a photograph. A snapshot was duly taken and the camera, with film intact and untouched inside, was handed to the Captain for safekeeping. No other camera was aboard the vessel, so no substitution was possible.

On reaching port the Captain handed the camera over to officials of the shipping company and they sent it directly to their New York office, where the film was developed and printed by a commercial photographer, and there were the heads of Courtney and Meehan, exactly as they had been seen on board ship! As Carrington himself described it, the two 'spirit extras' were 'remarkably clear' on the photograph – and recognized by people who knew the men in life. The photograph was taken by sceptical amateurs with a camera and film provided by others. Such was the accepted story, but the facts were a little different – as Carrington discovered.

The two men had certainly died and been buried at sea, and it seems indisputable that practically all the officers and seamen aboard ship saw the phantom heads, sometimes more than once, and often at the same time as others saw them. They appeared most frequently on the same side of the vessel as the side from which they had been cast overboard;

and they also appeared amid the waves near the ship. But there was no camera on board and no photograph was taken at that time. When the ship docked the Captain reported the case to his superiors. One of them produced a camera, another provided a sealed film, and these were in the custody of the Captain as he prepared for the *return* journey.

In the event the two phantom heads were repeatedly seen again, and the Captain inserted the film into the camera and took six exposures. When the ship again docked the Captain took the camera containing the film, which had not left his possession, to Mr James Patton, an officer of the company, who in turn took it with him to New York where it was developed by a commercial photographer.

TWO PHANTOM heads photographed from SS Watertown. *They were thought to be those of two seamen who died in an accident and were buried at sea*

The first five exposures showed no abnormality but on the sixth the heads of the two seamen were clear and sharp. Neither the shipping company, who at one time exhibited an enlarged copy of the photograph in the lobby of their New York office, nor Hereward Carrington, nor anyone else, has ever explained the picture – the original of which sadly must have disappeared. Carrington offered no theory but seemed to favour the possibility of 'thought-forms'.

There are those who believe that it is possible – consciously or unconsciously – to project thought-forms that can assume sufficient reality to appear in photographs. (Indeed there are those who think that most, if not all, ghosts are nothing more than thought-forms.) Twenty years ago experiments were conducted by Dr Jule Eisenbud and others into the 'thoughtographs' obtained in the vicinity of Chicago alcoholic Ted Serios. These seemed to show the places Serios had said he would think of, and he claimed to project his thoughts directly on to the film inside the polaroid camera. Some of the photographs, taken from an unusual angle – such as high in the air – were very curious and convincing, and some places could be identified from pictures in magazines or books. Much suspicion surrounded the use of what Serios called his 'gizmo' – a small cardboard tube which he would grasp and stare down towards the camera – but nothing was ever found, though the stigma of possible fraud remained. However, some Japanese parapsychologists have also produced similar impressive 'thoughtographs'.

THE BROWN LADY

With or without the somewhat vague photograph, taken in 1936, the ghostly Brown Lady of Raynham Hall, Fakenham, Norfolk, near the east coast of England, seat of the marquess of Townshend, has reportedly been seen on many occasions over the past 150 years. Many reports involve a figure moving quietly down the main staircase, along one of the corridors, and in and out of one of the first-floor bedrooms; a clear and distinct figure seemingly dressed in a gown of brown satin with yellow trimmings and a ruff around the throat. The features are quite clearly defined but the eyes are sometimes dark hollows and her cheeks have been described as unnaturally white. She is usually silent and harmless, but very occasionally there seems to be an evil, menacing quality about the haunting figure and sightings of her have been known to bring terror to those who experience them. This reaction may well rest with the witness and have nothing to do with the ghostly figure.

The ancient house that stood here was renovated by the Townshends when they purchased the property in the first half of the nineteenth century and one of the well-attested sightings of the famous Brown Lady occurred when Captain Frederick Marryat (1792-1848) came to stay. The son of a distinguished politician, he was a British naval captain and famous author of such books as *Mr Midshipman Easy* (1836), *Peter Simple* (1834) and *Masterman Ready* (1841). This knowledgeable and honest seaman always claimed to have encountered the Brown Lady during a visit to Raynham Hall in 1835, when he was among the guests of Lord and Lady Charles Townshend.

His host talked of reported sightings of the ghost and Marryat told his friend not to be upset by such tales. He said he did not believe in ghosts and if somebody was playing tricks he would welcome the opportunity of crossing swords with them!

Marryat occupied a large, first-floor, panelled room, containing a portrait of Dorothy Walpole, whose ghost the Brown Lady is thought to be. She was a direct blood relative of the Townshends, who lived unhappily at Raynham Hall suffering mental depression and spending the last years of her life confined to that particular room. Her brother was Sir Robert Walpole, England's Prime Minister in 1722. The sad Dorothy is supposed to be looking for her children, who had been taken away from her when she and her husband separated. There have also been stories that she either fell or was pushed to her death down the staircase that her ghost now haunts.

Before settling down for the night Marryat took the precaution of placing a loaded revolver under his pillow. The first night passed without incident, as did the second night, and the third night – except that just as he was about to retire, two nephews of Lord Charles Townshend, who were sharing a bedroom further down the corridor, asked him whether he would be good enough to give them his opinion on a new gun one of them had bought. The captain agreed, picked up a candle and, as an afterthought, took his loaded revolver and followed the two young men to their bedroom.

Having seen the gun and duly admired it Marryat prepared to return to his own room. The two young men said they would see him back there, so the three set off down the gloomy corridor together, only their footfalls breaking the silence of the quiet old house. They had gone only a few steps when the captain halted. 'Look. . .' he whispered. Moving towards them from the direction of Marryat's room was the figure of a woman, wearing a dress that rustled as she walked.

As the figure approached all three men noticed the temperature drop and Captain Marryat saw that the features of the figure closely resembled the portrait in his bedroom while the clothing matched that described to him by Lord Townshend. Thinking this must be someone playing at being the ghost he pointed his revolver at the figure, but it made no difference, and waiting until the figure was within feet of him, Captain Marryat fired his revolver point-blank at it! The noise in the confined space of the corridor was deafening and the three men waited for the smoke to clear, expecting to see a body. . . but the corridor was completely deserted. They all felt it might have been a hallucination, except that their description tallied and a bullet hole in the panelling of the corridor showed where the captain's bullet had gone through the figure they had all seen.

Not only did Captain Marryat always swear he had seen the Brown Lady, often being ridiculed for his trouble, but those who knew him best respected his one brush with a ghost. His daughter, Florence, believed implicitly in her father's story and recounted it in her volume of reminiscences, *There is No Death* (1891), ending her account with the words: 'My father never attempted again to interfere with the Brown Lady of Raynham Hall and I have heard that she haunts the premises to this day. That she did so at that time, however, there is no shadow of doubt.'

Some years ago a correspondent, Mrs Gladys Marshall of South Harrow, wrote to inform me that she had attended a school at West Raynham and for as long as she could remember all the children knew about the Brown Lady, and to tell me that she had slept at Raynham Hall, alone apart from Lady Joanna Townshend, in the 1960s. She said she had wandered all over the house, especially around midnight, wondering whether she would see anything but she never did. Mrs Marshall also told me she had seen a phantom horse, 'also connected with the Townshend family', on no less than three occasions.

THE GHOST of the Brown
Lady photographed at
Raynham Hall in Norfolk
for the English magazine
Country Life

She informed me that it was the Dowager Marchioness Townshend who had agreed to some photographers visiting Raynham Hall in 1936. She was interested in the subject of ghosts and quite fascinated by the resulting photograph. It was arranged that two top professional photographers, Captain Provand, art director of a Piccadilly firm of Court photographers, and his assistant Indre Shira, would visit the Hall and take photographs for *Country Life* magazine. On the morning of 19 September 1936 they duly arrived and took a large number of photographs of the house and grounds and then, at about four o'clock in the afternoon, they came to the oak staircase. Indre Shira described what happened next in *Country Life* dated 26 December 1936.

Captain Provand took one photograph of it while I flashed the light. He was focusing again for another exposure; I was standing by his side just behind the camera with the flashlight pistol in my hand, looking directly up the staircase.

All at once I detected an ethereal, veiled form coming slowly down the stairs. Rather excitedly I called out sharply: 'Quick! Quick! There's something! Are you ready?' 'Yes' the photographer replied, and removed the cap from the lens. I pressed the trigger of the flashlight pistol. After the flash, and on closing the shutter, Captain Provand removed the focusing cloth from his head and, turning to me, said: 'What's all the excitement about?'

I directed his attention to the staircase and explained that I had distinctly seen a figure there – transparent so that the steps were visible through the ethereal form, but nevertheless very definite and to me perfectly real. He laughed and said I must have imagined I had seen a ghost – for there was nothing now to be seen. It may be of interest to record that the flash from the Sasha bulb, which in this instance was used, is equivalent, I understand, to a speed of one-fiftieth part of a second.

After securing several other pictures, we decided to pack up and return to Town. Nearly all the way back we were arguing about the possibility of obtaining a genuine ghost photograph. Captain Provand laid down the law most emphatically by assuring me that as a Court photographer of thirty years' standing, it was quite impossible to obtain an authentic ghost photograph – unless, possibly, in a seance room – and in that connection he had had no experience.

I have neither his technical skill nor long years of practical experience as a portraitist, neither am I interested in psychic phenomena; but I maintained that the form of a very refined influence was so real to my eyes that it must have been caught at that psychological moment by the lens of the camera. . . .

When the negatives of Raynham Hall were developed, I stood beside Captain Provand in the dark-room. One after the other they were placed in the developer. Suddenly Captain Provand exclaimed: 'Good Lord! There's something on the staircase negative, after all!' I took one glance, called to him 'Hold it' and dashed downstairs to the chemist, Mr Benjamin Jones, manager of Blake, Sandford and Blake, whose premises are immediately underneath our studio. I invited Mr Jones to come upstairs to our dark-room. He came, and saw the negative just as it had been taken from the developer and placed in the adjoining hypo bath. Afterwards, he declared that, had he not seen for himself the negative being fixed, he would not have believed in the genuineness of the picture. Incidentally, Mr Jones has had considerable experience as an amateur photographer in developing his own plates and films.

Mr Jones, Captain Provand and I vouch for the fact that the negative has not been retouched in any way. It has been examined critically by a number of experts. No one can account for the appearance of the ghostly figure; but it is there clear enough. . . .

The much-reproduced Raynham Hall photograph is only one of many photographs that are alleged to depict spontaneous ghosts. Many can be dismissed as fraudulent (often double-exposure is blatantly obvious) and others are difficult to authenticate owing to the absence of witnesses. A remarkable photograph that does not appear to be faked (the negative was examined by Kodak and other experts) and where witnesses of impeccable standing have been named, interviewed and examined is the so-called Greenwich Ghost photograph. The circumstances under which a photograph is taken and the contemporary evidence are all-important and in these respects the Greenwich photograph is especially interesting and convincing.

THE GREENWICH GHOST

While on a visit to London in 1966 the Rev. and Mrs R W Hardy from White Rock, British Columbia, visited Greenwich and photographed the Tulip Staircase in the Queen's House. When the transparency was developed, after their return to Canada, a shrouded figure was clearly visible clutching the stairway rail; in fact it is possible to see two figures! (There were always attendants on duty in the vicinity of the Tulip Staircase to ensure that no one attempted to pass the barrier and climb the staircase, and to safeguard the many valuable paintings housed there.)

A GHOST photograph taken by the Rev. R W Hardy at the Queen's House, Greenwich, London. No one was visible at the time, or later, climbing the stairs. This photograph, and the original negative, have been examined by Kodak, and other photographic experts, who are totally unable to explain the shrouded figure; and there was certainly no double exposure

When the original photographic transparency came into the hands of the Ghost Club it was immediately submitted to Kodak and other experts, who all agreed that there was no trickery, or manipulation, or double-exposure, or any duplicity as far as the transparency was concerned; the only logical explanation they could offer was that there must have been someone on the stairs. Against this we have the evidence of the Rev. and Mrs Hardy, and the fact that the strict museum attendants would never countenance any dressing-up or playing about on the Tulip Staircase.

I have to say that, accepting the circumstances in which the photograph is said to have been taken and the good faith of everyone concerned, the Greenwich Ghost photograph is the most remarkable and interesting one I have seen in half a century of serious psychical investigation; and I have had some very interesting and puzzling photographs sent to me.

A PHOTOGRAPH taken at Rossal House, Sunbury-on-Thames, England, by Sherard Cowper-Coles, an electro-metallurgist, an engineer and inventor. His wife was also a scientist, and she actually saw the ghost that haunted the house. Cowper-Coles conducted a series of photographic experiments in company with Admiral Moore (a member of the Ghost Club). This photograph was taken under test conditions in daylight in the sitting-room where a vacant armchair, covered in pink and white striped chintz, stood by the window. There was no one else in the sitting-room and the transparent man has never been identified

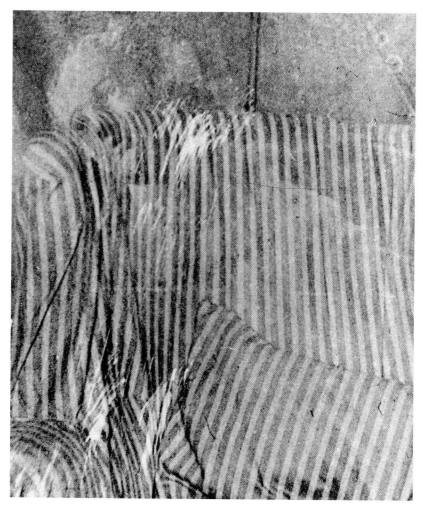

OTHER GHOST PHOTOGRAPHS

On 15 May 1982 Chris Brackley, a professional photographer from Banstead, Surrey, sent me a photograph of the interior of St Botolph's church, near Liverpool Street Station in the City of London. (See p.74.) In a covering letter he wrote:

My wife Carole and I had arranged to photograph a wedding at the church at 3.00 p.m. However, having arrived rather early (about 1.45 p.m.), we asked the cleaning lady if we could see inside the church before the guests arrived and this we were able to do, so we decided to take a couple of photographs of the interior while it was empty.

I should emphasise that no one else except my wife and myself were in the church at this time (the cleaning lady departed after unlocking the door for us). It was quite dark inside, with no artificial lighting; I therefore used a long exposure (approximately ten seconds) with my camera mounted on a tripod. The resulting print is enclosed and shows what appears to be the outline of a figure on the right balcony. I have no explanation for this. . . .

THE CHURCH and churchyard at Borley in Essex. The Rectory here became known as the most haunted house in England, until it was destroyed by fire in 1939, and four successive rectors, their wives and families, all asserted that they saw, heard and felt things they were totally unable to explain

A number of curious photographs that defy rational explanation have been taken at Borley in Essex, England. The churchyard there can be an awesome place. 'I was glad to get away' an experienced investigator once told me; and during a night I spent there four of us heard footsteps on the deserted gravel path. A *Picture Post* photograph taken by Thurston Hopkins in 1954 shows an unexplained 'black mist' that was not visible to the photographer or his companion.

For more than fifty years visitors have sought to photograph the site of 'the most haunted house in England' (where a ghost nun is said to have been seen by more than two dozen witnesses); the cottage that was once part of the Rectory property; the church just across the road (that must have been known to all the inhabitants of the haunted Rectory);

and the churchyard (where many of the actors in this unique drama lie buried); and even the road between the church and the Rectory site. Many photographers have found that their cameras malfunction, their light meters do not work or the resulting photograph shows an abnormality of some kind that seems to cry out for explanation.

SOME TIPS ON GHOST PHOTOGRAPHY

So it would appear that on occasions 'ghosts' or something 'inexplicable' can be caught on film. The obvious advice when visiting a haunted house or locality is always carry a camera and always take a few photographs – especially if you think you see a ghost! But there are one or two routine precautions that you should take in any attempt to catch a ghost with your camera. Do thoroughly search the area where you plan to take a photograph – the room, passage, stairway, corridor or open space – to ensure that there is nothing that might affect your photograph, and so that you can state categorically afterwards that you did search before taking the photograph. Secondly, do examine and prepare your equipment carefully: after the photograph is taken it is too late to say that perhaps the camera could have moved, or that light might possibly have reached the film other then through the lens.

Thirdly, you should keep a careful record of each exposure detailing the date, time, weather conditions, available light, exposure used, etc.

Infra-red photography can produce interesting results using a special filter that stops all but infra-red radiation, but only really works for the serious researcher. Exposure times can be difficult to estimate due to the quality of light at different times of the day, and such aspects as the amount of infra-red radiation and density of filter to be used have to be taken into account.

Cameras vary in their complexity, dexterity, sensitivity and automatic action but whether yours is one of the most sophisticated and expensive pieces of photographic equipment available, or the simplest and least expensive on the market, a camera is an indispensable part of the ghost hunter's equipment. As good and puzzling photographs have been obtained with reasonably-priced cameras as with the more expensive ones, though obviously automatic focusing and flash, the impossibility of double-exposure and so on add considerably to the usefulness of the ghost hunter's camera. 'Ghost' photographs are easily faked – and it is sometimes very difficult to decide which, if any, are genuine (in common with so much evidence that faces the psychical researcher) – nevertheless, some very convincing photographs have been obtained in near perfect conditions. So, since it would appear that there is always the possibility of obtaining a genuine 'ghost' photograph it is advisable for ghost hunters to have their cameras ready at all times in all places.

The majority of photographs purporting to depict spontaneous ghosts are not genuine, but a few are neither proved to be fakes nor can be attributed to some fault in the camera, the film or the taking of the photograph (double-exposure for example). There are in existence photographs apparently depicting ghosts which it is very difficult to explain in rational terms.

AMATEUR PHOTOGRAPHER Reginald Wickens thinks he may have obtained a photograph of the ghost of a swerving motorcyclist at Frome in Somerset, England, outside Morton House where three military dispatch riders were killed during the Second World War, and where Field Marshal Montgomery had his headquarters from June 1940. The obvious explanation for the photograph is that the shadow is that of the photographer, but the sun was almost directly overhead at the time, resulting in only a minimum shadow

$\mathcal{Ghosts}$

WHERE ARE THEY SEEN?

The question that everyone asks themselves sooner or later is: *where* can I see a ghost? And the simple answer is anywhere, for ghosts have been reported from every part of the world and in every situation.

Years ago, when I mentioned to a London bookseller the apparent rarity of ghosts, he looked askance at me and said, 'You walk about the streets of London, don't you? Half the people you see are ghosts!' I don't know about that, but I do think it is often the case that we see a ghost without being aware of the fact. Many spontaneous ghosts do appear to be solid and real, they act naturally and it is only in the light of later events or subsequent knowledge that one realizes one has seen a ghost. Often, of course, such later events do not occur and so we may never be sure of having seen a ghost or ghosts.

It is established, however, that some places are more haunted than others – or perhaps it is more correct to say that in some places there are a greater number of reported ghosts than in other places. There may be good reasons why this is so, and we are still seeking to explore them. They could include atmospheric pressure, climatic conditions and the presence of certain people. All these, and other possibilities, are being actively explored and investigated by psychic researchers all over the world.

'THE OLD Burlington' in Church Street, Chiswick, London, a former Elizabethan ale house haunted by a ghost in a wide-brimmed black hat

THE MOST HAUNTED CITY IN EUROPE

Certainly there are towns and villages regarded as being particularly haunted. York, in the north of England, has often claimed to be Britain's most haunted town for example. The *Guinness Book of Records* has even called York 'the most haunted city in Europe', so perhaps a visit to York is advisable for those who wish to see ghosts.

In any case, the city of York is well worth a visit with its 2½-mile walk along the top of the fourteenth-century city walls; its Micklegate Bar, where the heads of traitors used to be displayed after execution; its Cathedral, built on the site of the building where the first Christian King of Northumbria was baptized in 627; its Clifford's Tower, built

TREASURER'S HOUSE in York is the scene of the remarkable and periodic appearance of a troop of Roman soldiers, led by a mounted centurion, who are only visible above the knees. They are evidently marching on the old Roman road, which ran below the level of the present cellar flooring

YORK HAS the reputation, of being one of Europe's most haunted towns. This is York Minster, which has at least two ghosts, seen from the city walls

by William the Conqueror in 1068; its Castle Museum, housing three entire period streets lined with shops; and its narrow streets, Shambles and Stonegate, barely changed since medieval days.

A tour of the ghosts of York (where I presided at the original Ghost Weekend in 1974) must surely start at the Treasurer's House, built on Roman foundations, though the present structure dates mainly from the seventeenth and eighteenth centuries with thirteenth-century work in the undercroft. From a psychic point of view Treasurer's House claims some spectacular ghosts. It was once the home of the powerful Aislabie family and George Aislabie, mortally wounded in a duel in 1674, died here, where his ghost has continued to haunt for more than 300 years. The Tapestry Room on the first floor was once the scene of murder in the nineteenth century and many people have sensed a gloomy and forbidding influence here which, on occasions, builds up into a phantom form.

The most remarkable and famous ghost story associated with the house, however, was first related to me by Harry Martindale, later a policeman, but a plumber's apprentice in 1953 when he worked in the cellars of the Treasurer's House helping to install central heating. One morning, as he stood on a short ladder, he suddenly heard the sound of a trumpet. A moment later he heard the sound again, but nearer; and then again, louder and closer still. The next minute he saw the figure of a horse come through the wall, huge and lumbering, carrying a man on its back – a soldier in Roman costume!

Shocked and confused Harry fell to the earth floor and watched, wide-eyed, as the mounted soldier was followed by a group of foot-soldiers carrying lances, round shields and short-bladed swords, and wearing plumed Roman helmets. They walked dejectedly forward, shuffling and dispirited, with their heads bowed, a dozen or more in all; and then Harry noticed that they appeared to be cut off at the knees! (Later excavations revealed that the soldiers must have been walking at the original level of a Roman road that once ran here.)

As the whole group silently disappeared into the opposite wall the shocked young man rushed out of the cellars and up to the ground floor, where he bumped into the Museum Curator, who said, before Harry Martindale had a chance to speak: 'You've seen the Romans, haven't you?' It seemed that a female visitor had also seen the arresting spectacle, as had a previous Museum Curator in 1946, and a visiting American professor in the 1930s; while a young lady attending a fancy dress party in the 1920s had suddenly found her passage barred by a Roman soldier. When he did not respond to her requests to move she turned on her heel and returned upstairs where she discovered there was no one dressed like the 'man' she thought she had seen. The present curator holds statements from other witnesses who also claim to have seen the ghostly legion.

Harry Martindale told me he had been questioned by many people about his experience, including experts in Roman history, and they had been much impressed by his description of the Roman soldiers, including the *round* shields they carried. These would suggest they belonged to the later part of the first century, possibly remnants of the somewhat mysterious Ninth Legion.

Nor are these ghosts the only ones that might be encountered at the Treasurer's House, while elsewhere in York there are many reported phantoms. York Minster has the ghost of a man called Dean Gale, who sits in his old pew, and of a medieval wood carver (seen in 1972). The ghosts of a 'tall and graceful' young woman and a young nursemaid and her charge haunt Holy Trinity Church (where the churchyard is also haunted by several ghosts). The Theatre Royal has a frequently-seen Grey Lady and the unexplained sound of chanting – possibly associated with the thirteenth-century hospital serviced by nuns that once stood on the site. The Grey Lady was seen by actress Evelyn Laye in 1975, and by directors and other actors and actresses on many occasions – most of them never having heard of the Grey Lady until they saw her.

The City Library has the ghost of an unidentified old man and St William's College that of a little old lady (last seen in 1978) as well as pacing footsteps that are thought to be those of a murderer. A small house in College Street (No. 5) has the ghost of a little girl who starved to death there in the seventeenth century. The public houses in York which claim ghosts include the Cock and Bottle (the ghost of George Villiers, the evil 1st Duke of Buckingham, favourite of James I); the Black Swan (a small, miserable-looking man, a young woman with beautiful hair and a pair of disembodied male legs); the Windmill Hotel ('an icy mist'); and the York Arms, which has a pleasant old lady who opens and closes doors and interferes with various objects.

Then there is King's Manor with its ghost monk and a woman dressed in green (thought to be Anne Boleyn), while the ghost of Charles I haunts the stone stairway leading to the Huntingdon Room – and the King was certainly here in 1636, 1639 and 1642. Various odd experiences have also been reported from houses in the older parts of York, the Shambles and historic Bedern, and even in the Coppergate Shopping Centre, where poltergeist activity was repeatedly experienced a few years ago in one of the modern shops.

FARNHAM, ENGLAND

Another candidate for 'most haunted town' must be Farnham in Surrey, about forty miles south-west of London, where a police officer became interested in local ghost sightings and soon collected fifty first-hand reports!

There is a picturesque and historic Castle that still dominates the town at the top of Castle Street and visitors to it have included William of Wykeham, Lord High Chancellor of England and founder of New College, Oxford in 1379; Cardinal Beaufort, half-brother of Henry IV,

England's first Lancastrian king from 1399 to 1413, and one of those who saw Joan of Arc burned in the market-place at Rouen in France; Cardinal Wolsey, builder of Hampton Court Palace and Henry VIII's Lord Chancellor; Henry VIII himself; his daughters Mary I (on her way to marry Philip of Spain at Winchester) and Elizabeth I; and James I, George III and Queen Victoria. There are also several well-attested ghosts.

The gateway to the great Norman keep, built by King Stephen's brother, Henry of Blois, who became Bishop of Winchester in 1129, is haunted by an indistinct form that many visitors have found positively frightening. Some have said they caught a glimpse of a stern-faced lady in a light-coloured gown with a cord girdle, perhaps twelfth or thirteenth century, and there have been whispers of intrigue and dark deeds here long ago – even murder – that might have left some lingering impression, reflection or vibration.

The present castle has a ghost monk in the Great Hall and ghostly clangs of a non-existent bell in the Fox Tower, where the ghost of Bishop Morley has been seen and heard. He restored the castle after the Restoration of Charles II and lived for years in a small cell-like room in Fox Tower, where he slept in a coffin. There is also a phantom dancing girl on the stairway outside the Great Hall; a grey-robed silent figure haunts another of the stairways on sunny afternoons; unexplained footsteps appear to traverse the older parts of the castle and the steep hill leading to the entrance; and an indefinite shape crouches in the corner of one bedroom.

Castle Street itself has its ghosts: a phantom coach has been seen to pull up and a dandy to alight and swagger across the wide street to disappear into one of the Regency houses, where he is said to have strangled his mistress. The old Castle Theatre premises there also have the reputation for being haunted by a murderer, and there are witnesses who saw and heard seemingly inexplicable happenings when the rambling building was an active theatre with dressing rooms – and a property room full of costumes and stage props where a man was once found hanged. One evening there I was introduced to the English stage and film actor, the late Sir Michael Redgrave (after whom a new theatre in Farnham was named) and he told me that he had performed in many haunted theatres but, for his money, the Castle Theatre beat them all! (Another theatre that aspiring ghost hunters should undoubtedly visit is the Theatre Royal, in Drury Lane, London. If you can visit the theatre and walk about the stalls, stage and upper circle, as I have, when the theatre is deserted, you will have a never-to-be-forgotten experience, and even if you don't meet the famous Man in Grey (see pp.95-6) you will see his habitat and locale.)

Among the haunted private houses in Farnham is a property in East Street where the figure of a female has been seen in the doorway of a bedroom, dressed in an old-fashioned full-skirted dress. She is possibly a long-forgotten nanny, for sightings have almost invariably been

ANOTHER HAUNTED British theatre is the Theatre Royal in Bath, where a ghostly Grey Lady haunts. She is thought to have been the cause of a duel and she committed suicide when the wrong man won. The Garrick's Head is connected to the theatre by a once secret passage and one of the duellists is glimpsed there from time to time

reported when some member of the family occupying the house is expecting a child. Another house not far away has two ghosts, one that of a fair young lady and the other of a dashing young man.

A shop in West Street has a ghostly black dog that has been seen spontaneously over a period of fifty years by various occupants and visitors, many of the latter completely unaware of the reported ghost. Here, too, there is the phantom form of an old woman, standing still and mournful in a room that is now a bathroom. Also, a curious sound has occasionally been heard that has been likened to a roll of drums – that may or may not be of ghostly origin. Another shop, once a famous jeweller's, who held a Royal Charter, used to be – and perhaps still is – sometimes visited by the ghost of the long-dead founder. He was seen by several workmen when the premises were being modernized a few years ago.

Elsewhere in West Street a ghostly little old lady wearing an eighteenth-century mob-cap hobbles at incredible speed. She keeps

FARNHAM PARISH church in Surrey, England, where ghostly chanting has been heard. There is also a ghostly procession and a female figure, who has entered the church on many occasions – and then disappeared

very close to the houses bordering the road and suddenly disappears into one of the doorways. She has most frequently been seen on wet nights during the winter months.

The Ranger's House in Farnham Park harbours the ghost of a pretty young girl but no one seems to know who she is or why she haunts. Some years ago I talked with the then owner who knew all about the ghost but had never seen her. 'Perhaps I look too hard . . .' she said.

A jeweller's in Lion and Lamb courtyard, which has been restored and developed with shops, was once a restaurant haunted by a lady in grey who had been seen scores of times by staff and customers. The quiet, gentle-looking little old lady appeared to be completely solid and normal until, usually when she was about to be served, she was no longer there. At one time there were reports of the figure being seen several times during the course of one day, then she would not be seen for months. Facing the restaurant, near an ancient lead pump, a young woman in old-fashioned dress used to be seen standing in what was once the yard of an inn. After the pump was moved a little way to make room for a modern shop, reports of the ghostly figure dwindled.

The parish church in Farnham has several ghosts, including that of a little old lady who was occasionally seen entering the porch around the time of evensong but who was never seen inside the church. Some witnesses said they virtually followed the figure into the church, she had been only a few steps ahead of them, but inside the church there was no sign of her. The Rev. Allan Wheeler was a curate there and he informed me that he had seen the figure on several occasions. 'Believe me,' he said. 'I thought she was absolutely real and so did a colleague who was with me on one occasion.' More than once inside the church a churchwarden has found himself addressing a phantom priest; and sounds like horses champing and pawing the ground have been heard from the rear of the church, which is interesting because Oliver Cromwell used the church as stables during the English Civil War when skirmishes were fought in the area.

The sound of Latin chanting, apparently emanating from the nave, has been reported quite recently as well as fifty years ago by a Second-World-War fire-watcher. In 1960 a visitor, alone in the church, felt that the building was suddenly full of people, and she says she watched a gold-clad celebrant accompanied by brightly-clad assistants take part in a pre-Reformation (Catholic) High Mass. She clearly saw and smelt the incense smoke and at any moment expected to hear music or chanting, but the whole scene was enacted in total silence. Suddenly the church door opened and she turned to see the rector enter accompanied by a friend; when she looked back towards the altar all the people had disappeared and the church was deserted.

A modern police station now stands hard by an equally modern bridge over the River Wey at Farnham. Once this Longbridge, as it was called, was the final obstacle for a tired coachman, his passengers and the horses before a welcome stop at the inn that used to stand

BOURNE MILL is one of many haunted properties in Farnham, England. A ghost lady in a crinoline has been seen here on a stairway

nearby, known as the Adam and Eve, later the Hop Bag Inn, and later still The Downing Street. Longbridge was well-known for the phantom coach and horses that used to clatter over the bridge and turn swiftly into the yard of the inn. It may be that all that remains of this haunting are the sounds that once accompanied it, for in recent times the noise of a coach and horses had been heard here, and at the inn visitors used to be awakened by the sound of panting horses, the grind of heavy wheels and the clank of harness, although nothing was visible.

Also in Farnham there is a restaurant in West Street where the stairs are haunted by an unidentified couple, a man in the uniform of the Duke of Wellington's day, who has been glimpsed near the entrance and a girl from a similar age who has been seen near the rear of the premises. The ancient Bush Hotel, an alehouse in the thirteenth century, has a bedroom reputed to be haunted by an old-time serving maid – she was seen a few years ago by a girl occupying the room on the eve of her wedding. She said the ghost looked friendly and seemed to smile before 'melting into nothingness'.

A picturesque mill at Farnham, now an antiques market, has a ghostly lady in a crinoline who haunts a stairway and a Victorian lady haunts a Victorian cottage in Waverley Lane. Farm buildings on the outskirts of the town harbour yet another female phantom and a former malt-house where malt was prepared and stored for brewing is haunted by the ghost of a head malt-master who was drowned in a vat.

Charles I stayed at Vernon House on his way to trial in London, where he was found guilty of treason and beheaded in 1649, and the room he occupied is haunted. Reports of paranormal activity there go back many years. Nearby a ghost train has been seen on the old Runfold track that has long disappeared, and a phantom Roman army marches up the hill south of the town where many Roman coins have been unearthed. There are other ghosts in Farnham, but perhaps I have recounted sufficient to whet the appetite of ghost hunters.

There are reportedly haunted houses in practically every town throughout the world, but some are more haunted than others. By the same token many villages have ghosts and hauntings, but a few villages have a *wealth* of hauntings within their precincts.

THE MOST HAUNTED VILLAGE IN ENGLAND

Pluckley in Kent, on the way from London to Folkestone, has the reputation of being the most haunted village in England and certainly it has many reported ghosts, from the phantom White Lady of the Derings to a creepy churchyard. The local rector Rev. John Pittock has not repudiated all ghost sightings in the village and, in particular, those in and around the church of St Nicholas where the Red Lady has been reportedly seen by visitors and local people and where the Dering Chapel has been the scene of curious knocks and unexplained lights. The churchyard, too, has been the subject of frequent reports concerning a ghostly 'woman in white' and a phantom white dog.

THIS IS the haunted church of St Nicholas in Pluckley in Kent, England. The ghost of the beautiful Lady Dering, buried here in the Dering Chapel with a red rose at her breast, has been seen walking in the churchyard – resplendent in her finery and with a red rose at her bosom

Here at Pluckley where, understandably, some of the inhabitants have grown weary of ghost-hunting visitors and play down the subject of ghosts, there is a formidable selection: the Screaming Man; the Watercress Lady; a coach-and-pair; in fact, more than a dozen different ghosts have been reported reliably from this village. There is a cottage haunted by the ghost of a Victorian girl; a more substantial house haunted by the ghost of an elderly lady; and a phantom man who haunts Elvey Farm, where many strange happenings have been experienced. Greystones, now part of Rose Farm, has a brown-habited monk (seen within the last few years); Rose Court has a Tudor lady ghost; the crossroads near the Blacksmith's Arms are haunted by a highwayman killed in a fight there; near Cliff Cottage the ghost of a schoolmaster who hanged himself has been seen; a ruined mill is haunted by a former miller; a soldier, known as The Colonel, who committed suicide in Park Wood, walks again on dark nights; and there are various 'grey shapes', unidentified phantoms, and 'icy chills' in many of Pluckley's houses and cottages.

PLUCKLEY IS possibly England's most haunted village, and Greystones is one of the many haunted houses there

ANOTHER CONTESTANT

In recent years Prestbury, near Cheltenham, in the Cotswolds, has vied with Pluckley for the title of 'most haunted village in Britain', and there are at least twenty tales of hauntings in the village that warrant serious consideration.

A well-known ghost is the Black Abbot whose wanderings, especially it seems at Easter, Christmas and on All Souls' Day, cover a wide area of the village taking in the church, the grounds of the old Priory, the site of the Bishop's Palace, several cottages and the main village street. Then there is the phantom white horse and its medieval rider, last seen in 1989, and another ghostly horse and horseman that may date from the days of the English Civil War; while a similar but headless apparition was reportedly seen in 1971. Several cottages apparently have their individual and recognized ghosts, one being seen by six people in 1961. Sometimes the figures are accompanied by unexplained sounds: voices, footsteps, music, singing; and by equally inexplicable sights: moving shadows, strange lights and doors opening and closing by themselves.

A White Lady walks in the churchyard; a man in a fawn-coloured overcoat, but with no visible legs or face, has been seen in Mill Street (most recently in 1982), where the sound of marching feet has been reported from a deserted road. A ghostly old woman gathers sticks in front of one cottage, while a bedroom in another is haunted by the ghost of a burglar. There is also a 'leering' monk and an unidentified and undescribed man who haunts the old racecourse, where an old-fashioned funeral cortège has been seen. In Bruncer's Lane a mysterious 'glowing' figure has been reported and in the High Street the ghost of a lady in old-fashioned dress has been encountered, as well as a man described as a jockey and a young man on a motorcycle. So perhaps a visit to Prestbury is indicated, although many of the ghost reports there seem to depend on single, uncorroborated testimony.

ANOTHER HAUNTED VILLAGE

BORIS KARLOFF, the horror actor, whose unmistakable figure is said to haunt his last home at Bramshott in England

Another English village with numerous reported ghosts is Bramshott – not far from Farnham, but in Hampshire, where the old manor house (I was told when I was there) is haunted by three ghosts: an Elizabethan priest; an early Quaker; and a White Lady, thought to be Lady Hole, a former owner.

Here are also the ghost of a gamekeeper named Adams; the phantom form of someone called Elizabeth Butler, who drowned herself in 1745 and still walks beside the slow-moving stream; and a ghostly girl who comes out of the church wearing a poke bonnet and disappears through the churchyard wall, where a Grey Lady is seen beside another wall where she committed suicide. There is also a ghostly pot-boy who disappears almost as soon as he is seen; a group of Tudor ghosts who haunt a leafy lane of the village; a party of women and children from a later time who haunt a lodge house; a phantom coach and horses has been known to clatter through the village; a mounted Cavalier rides through a hedge; and a murdered highwayman is borne silently along a lane on the back of his faithful horse. Other phantom animals here include a black pig and a white calf-like creature about the size of a large cat! And, on a more prosaic note, the unmistakable figure of tall and bow-legged Boris Karloff – who played the monster in *Frankenstein* (1931) – has been seen in the vicinity of Roundabout, the cottage he loved towards the end of his life.

OTHER HAUNTED PLACES

In France a visit to the Palace of Versailles and its environs could well be productive. Here, two distinguished scholars always swore they stepped back into the past one August day in 1901 and found themselves amid gardens and buildings and people at Versailles before the French Revolution of 1789. Since then there have been many reports of other visitors encountering supernormal activity, including historical figures – especially in the vicinity of the Petit Trianon, the little retreat that Louis XVI presented to his queen, the ill-fated Marie Antoinette.

In San Diego, California, the Villa Montezuma has a curious, haunted reputation. Known locally as the Spook House, tragedy upon tragedy seems to have left its mark on this brooding Victorian mansion with its haunted Music Room and onion-shaped tower – and the sobbing ghost who haunts the upper rooms. Four successive owners lived in terror here before the house passed into the hands of the City of San Diego in 1972. It is now a museum and many visitors still describe apparitions and unexpected shapes they glimpse from time to time in the numerous mirrors there. Even the guides, familiar with every part of the property, admit to feeling ghostly presences.

ST JAMES Hotel, Cimarron, New Mexico, a corner of the Old West, where twenty-six people died violently in the late 1880s – including five in one day – and where numerous inexplicable happenings have been reported, especially in Room 18 where there is a 'not so friendly' ghost

Elsewhere in America, in late 1991, curious happenings were being reported from the elegant St James Hotel, Cimarron, New Mexico. Over the years many odd and varied incidents have been reported there: birds dropping dead; objects moving or disappearing; bolts on doors slamming shut; glassware floating; and one visitor knocked to her knees.

The history of the St James shows that twenty-six people died there violently in the late 1880s – including five people in one day – and bullet holes still pockmark the dining-room ceiling. A former part-owner of the hotel, Pat Loree, a gynaecologist, has revealed that one night in 1986 she was showing Room 18 to Dr Kenneth Wright of Fresno when she encountered 'something' that she described as a 'not-so-friendly ghost' coming at her out of the room. 'It came down on me and passed me on my right and I felt like I was being struck at,' she said in 1991. 'I fell to my knees . . . I got back up and at that point it came back at me and knocked me back to my knees and went to the corner of the room where it seemed to spin and swirl. . . .'

THE VIEW from inside The White House in Washington DC, where well-authenticated ghost sightings include Abraham Lincoln, Abigail Adams, Dolly Madison and Willie Lincoln, who died while his father was president

Room 18 is now closed to the public. Hardly larger than a walk-in closet, it contains only a dusty oak bedframe without a mattress. The present owner-manager, Ed Sitzberger, explains: 'We've never had anybody sleep in there – not with the things that are going on. . . .'

Then, if you have the requisite entrée, there is always Washington's White House, where several ghost forms have been sighted reliably over the years. The ghost of Abraham Lincoln, in particular, has been seen and sensed by successive occupants – and by some distinguished visitors, including Queen Wilhelmina of the Netherlands. Franklin Delano Roosevelt felt, on many occasions, that Lincoln was present with him in the Blue Room; his wife Eleanor always believed the Lincoln Room to be haunted and several visitors and staff, including a maid called Mary Eban, claimed to see the figure of Lincoln in that room. Another maid, Katurah Brooks, saw the unmistakable form of Lincoln in the Rose Room and the same figure has been seen walking through the East Room and standing at the window of the Oval Room.

Other well-attested ghosts at the White House include the phantom form of William Henry Harrison (ninth president of the United States), who died only a month after inauguration; Dolly Madison, wife of the fourth president, whose spectral appearance apparently succeeded in preventing the removal of her precious rose gardens; Abigail Adams (wife of the second president and mother of the sixth) has been seen and positively identified passing through the doors of the East Room; Lincoln's son Willie, who died prematurely, has reportedly been seen by several trusted members of the White House staff; and it even seems that Lucky, Ronald Reagan's dog, used to bark at the ghost of Abe Lincoln whenever he entered Honest Abe's bedroom.

Having decided where you are most likely to see a ghost – although you could see a spontaneous ghost just about anywhere – the next thing to think about is *when* you are most likely to see one.

HOLLYWOOD MEMORIAL Park Cemetery, the last resting place of actors like Peter Lorre and Peter Finch. The ghost of Clifton Webb (above), *star of* Laura, The Razor's Edge *and* Sitting Pretty, *all of which he received Oscar nominations for, still haunts the vicinity and has become one of Hollywood's most famous ghosts*

Ghosts

WHEN ARE THEY SEEN?

THE RUINS of Bramber Castle, Sussex, England, where the pathetic ghosts of the children of William de Breose have been seen regularly at Christmas time

Many so-called cyclic ghosts – those ghosts reputed to recur in regular cycles, usually annually – also sometimes occur at predestined times. For the benefit of ghost hunters everywhere I have compiled a new Ghost Calendar, detailing the dates on which cyclic ghosts are reputed to appear, as well as recounting some interesting hauntings. I have often wondered whether there is anything in the idea that witnesses to cyclic apparitions feed those apparitions and give them 'power' to appear again and again. Whatever brings them back, cyclic ghosts appear all over the world: some at certain times of year or in particular months; others on specific days or at special times of day. (See also p 26.)

One of the more unusual cyclic appearances in Britain is the ghostly three-masted schooner, *Lady Luvibond*, lost with all hands on 13 February, 1748, on the treacherous Goodwin Sands off the town of Deal on the Kent coast. Every fifty years *Lady Luvibond* is said to re-enact her last journey. She was seen in 1798 by the master of the *Edenbridge*, who entered the sighting in his log-book, and she was seen at the same time by the crew of a fishing vessel.

In 1848 long-shoremen from Deal saw the phantom ship aground and went to take part in a rescue operation, but no trace of any ship was found. In 1898 shore watchers again saw a schooner sailing straight for the sands; and in 1948 there were claims that she had been seen yet again, and dead on schedule.

The original *Lady Luvibond* sailed for Oporto, Portugal, out of London with the captain's new wife aboard, and a first mate who had been a rival for the affections of the bride. It seems that in a fit of jealousy the mate killed the helmsman and then deliberately sailed the *Lady Luvibond* onto the sands with the death of all on board. Her next appearance is due in 1998.

At Jenkyn Place, a Queen Anne house in Bentley in Hampshire, just west of Farnham, the ghost of a former housekeeper, known as 'Mrs Waggs', appears each February as she has been doing for the past half-century, at least – but not at any regular time, although she tends to favour the afternoon. She has certainly been seen within recent years by many members of the family and by visitors.

Orme House, in the middle of Newport, Isle of Wight, off the south coast of England, was once three small cottages. Today, in an area rebuilt in the 1700s, the ghost of an elderly lady in eighteenth-century clothes – long skirt, bodice, shawl and little leather boots – has been seen by residents; but only on 9 April and usually in the early hours. She was reportedly seen in 1985 and again in 1992.

At dawn each year on 17 May a phantom army is said to materialize on a small plain on the south coast of Crete, near the Venetian fortress of Frangocastello. During one of the fiercest battles of the Greek War of Independence in 1828, 385 Greeks were slaughtered here, to the last man, by a much larger Turkish force.

Then there is the mysterious and ghostly lady in pink who appears every two years in Yorba Family Cemetery at Yorba, San Diego, California. She comes on 15 June and her most favoured time is 5 p.m. Often the appearance of this ghost is heralded by interference with electrical or specialist equipment: walkie-talkies, cameras, flashlights and light meters.

The night of 5 July is the anniversary of the battle of Sedgemoor in Somerset, England. It was fought in 1685 shortly after the accession of James II, when Charles II's illegitimate son led a rebellion. Psychic manifestations have often been reported over the marshy battlefields: strange balls of light; shadowy figures; phantom horsemen; and ghostly troops are seen. The latter apparently flee silently through the neighbouring lanes towards the River Carey – just as they fled the place of battle more than 300 years ago. Some visitors have also heard the distant sound of battle.

The lonely Pacheco Pass in central California has also seen terrible times with battles involving American Indians, Spaniards, Mexicans and American settlers; and it is said that even today the nameless horror lurking there is responsible for the high number of road accidents. One California Highway Patrol officer asserted recently: 'I know people who won't drive through Pacheco Pass because they're

LOUGH LEANE, Killarney in Co. Kerry, where the Irish hero O'Donoghue is said to return at dawn each 1 May mounted on his favourite white horse

scared . . .'. Scores of visitors speak of awful feelings, being frightened of they know not what or having the impression of being alone and trapped, and many of their affidavits are preserved at the Nirvana Foundation. Often these feelings seem to be especially strong on September evenings between the hours of seven and nine, perhaps the time when something happened long ago that has left behind feelings and energy that are evident to this day.

EACH 1 November, the ghost of Sir John Jocelyn, mounted on his white steed, is said to ride furiously down the carriage drive of his old home, Hyde Hall, Sawbridgeworth, England (now a school), where he and his favourite white horse were buried together

The battle of Edgehill in 1642, where 14,000 Englishmen fought each other during the English Civil War, is another recurring psychic battle. There are scores of witnesses who aver to hearing the sounds of battle and to seeing bands of weary soldiers on this hilly ridge in Warwickshire each 23 October.

Another battle-related haunting is that of six ghostly members of the unpopular Prussian Field Marshal Blücher's family. They were killed in the Seven Years' War (1756–62), fought by France, Austria and Russia against Britain and Prussia, and are reputed to reappear once a year at midnight on 12 August – the date that Blücher himself also died in 1819, having helped the Duke of Wellington to defeat Napoleon.

My friend Herbert Greenhouse of New York tells me that Pawley's Island, off the mainland of South Carolina, is haunted. It can be a pleasant enough place in calm weather, but violent storms occasionally arise there with little or no warning, and it is in the direct path of hurricanes roaring along the coast from the Caribbean. The island has, in fact, been devastated by three classic storms, in 1822, 1893 and 1954. On each occasion a ghost known locally as the Grey Man was reportedly seen. He is regarded as the guardian ghost of the island and his appearance invariably warns of approaching gale winds or a violent storm. There is evidence that he has been watching over Pawley's Island for 150 years, and legends about him go back even further. His favoured months for haunting (when storms are also most likely) are late September and October.

A church in Millvale, Pennsylvania, is haunted by a dark-robed monk, late at night each mid-November. I heard about this haunting from Dr Oskar Goldberg, an international parapsychologist. Dr Goldberg had seen the mysterious figure himself, as had a mural painter working in the church, and a former rector, Father Zagar, together with other witnesses whom the priest had invited to watch for the ghost with him. They saw him for a few seconds as he walked past.

Elsewhere in America the Stevenson House Museum in Monterey State Park, central California, has a ghostly woman in black who is only seen during the first half of December each year, in the atmospheric nursery, around 4.30 p.m.; possibly a former nurse or mother returning to the place where once she knew happiness – or unhappiness – with a child.

One of the most popular days for cyclic ghosts has always been 31 October – Hallowe'en or All Saints' Eve. You might see a First World War soldier at Bournemouth Town Hall in south England; a hound and a huntsman at Cliviger Gorge near Burnley, Lancashire, in the north of England; the chiming of ghost bells and a phantom dog at Armboth Fell in Cumbria – the Lake District; six hooded figures in St Rita's Church, Chicago; and a solitary ghost monk walking the ruins of Minsden Chapel in Hertfordshire, just north of London.

Another popular day is 24 December, Christmas Eve, when the ghost of Anne Boleyn walks at Hever Castle in Kent; a phantom monk wanders among the ruins of Strata Florida Abbey in Dyfed, Wales; a ghostly coach and horses visits Roos Hall at Beccles in Suffolk, East Anglia; the spectral form of the Victorian novelist Dickens haunts the burial ground in the shadows of Rochester Castle in Kent – a place he had always loved and often visited; and a long-lost sanctus bell is heard ringing from the depths of Bomere Pool near Shrewsbury in Shropshire.

Sandringham in Norfolk, near the north coast of East Anglia, one of the fine country residences of England's royal family, and where several monarchs have died, is haunted each Christmas Eve. According to servants with years of service, and to other inhabitants, guests and visitors, Christmas cards are frequently thrown onto the floor and unoccupied beds are interfered with just before Christmas. The most

WHEN THE ghost of Sir Walter Raleigh returns to his old home, Sherborne Castle in Dorset, England, each St Michael's Eve (28 September), it usually visits the stone seat known as Raleigh's Seat

haunted area is the footman's corridor on the second floor, and maids often refuse to go there alone at this time of the year – they clean and dust in small groups. Even so, they and others have reported thudding footsteps echoing in the deserted passage, doors opening without anyone touching them and a very frightening sound which has been likened to 'a huge, grotesque lung breathing in and out'.

New Year's Eve, 31 December, is another popular date for cyclic ghosts. The long-vanished manor house of Knighton Gorges, on the Isle of Wight, off the south coast of England, is said to reappear each New Year's Eve at dusk. There are many witnesses who report the complete materialization of the haunted Elizabethan mansion, or of apparitions or inexplicable scenes on the site on New Year's Eve as far back as 1915 and as recently as 1982 and 1991.

Although a mild New Year's Eve will usually find a group of would-be ghost watchers in the vicinity, there are reports from people with no knowledge of the curious manifestation who happened to be in the area at the right time on the right date, and who saw the magnificent house – ablaze with lights and echoing distant music – before the whole thing faded away before their eyes.

Even parts of the old house, which was dismantled, are said to be haunted. A staircase used in the eighteenth century by the likes of John Wilkes, the outspoken English politician, the English actor David Garrick and the society portrait painter Sir Joshua Reynolds, and now incorporated into Langbridge House, Newchurch (less than a mile from its former home), is reportedly haunted by the bent and hooded figure of an elderly friar who is seen from time to time.

The poet and writer Robert Graves, an enthusiastic ghost observer, once told me that he invariably shared a glass of whisky with a ghost who always showed up on New Year's Eve at a house he knew in North Wales. When I asked him where the liquid that the ghost imbibed went, he said he really didn't know, but neither did he know where ghosts come from or where they go – and nor did anyone else . . .

But there can surely be nothing to beat the tradition that all the ghosts in Britain meet on the longest night of the year, 21 December, at the Stiper Stones near Bishop's Castle, Shropshire – yet I have never met anyone who has seen them, or even a few of them!

There are some ghost who are not governed by dates but seem to appear on certain days, or times of day, at any time of the year. Another Isle of Wight ghost, at Rose Cottage in Roud near Godshill, often manifests in one way or another, but always on a Friday. There have been ghostly figures: that of a little girl in one of the bedrooms and that of a monk walking up and down the staircase; and there have been other seemingly quite inexplicable happenings – but only on Fridays. Oddly enough, a cottage at Brighstone Farm, also on the island, is haunted by a phantom blacksmith who still works at his anvil, judging by the loud sounds heard by owners, occupants and ghosts,

but only on Friday or Saturday nights. As often happens in genuine hauntings, the sounds, although loud and vibrating, are confined to the haunted room and are not heard in adjoining cottages.

I conducted an extensive survey over a ten-year period, taking into account ghost sightings reported from all parts of the world. The results reveal that the majority were seen during the hours of darkness: 54 per cent against 46 per cent. Of those seen during the hours of darkness 78 per cent were seen during the early hours – between 4.00 a.m. and 6.00 a.m. – when, perhaps, many people are between deep sleep and full awakeness. A great number (66 per cent) are also reported around the midnight hour – popularly regarded as the time to see ghosts as compared with any other hour of the day or night.

Ghosts known to the percipient compared with those who were unrecognized came out at 38 per cent against 62 per cent. Animal ghosts, either alone or accompanied by 'human beings', were seen by 32 per cent of those questioned; while only 14 per cent reported any sounds at the time of the sighting, against 86 per cent who reported complete silence. An overwhelming majority, 83 per cent, reported feeling cold, a sudden drop in temperature or a sudden chill at the time of the sighting, but this could well be a psychological reaction.

One of London's most famous ghosts, the Man in Grey, who haunts the Theatre Royal in Drury Lane, is a daytime ghost – he is never seen at night. He appears to be the ghost of a man murdered in the theatre in the seventeenth century, for in 1848 a skeleton with a Cromwellian-

THE WORLD'S most haunted theatre is the Theatre Royal in Drury Lane, London. Its Man in Grey is a daylight ghost and has been seen by literally scores of people

pattern dagger in its ribs was discovered in a tiny room. The ghost has been seen by literally hundreds of people during the last twenty years. Once, theatre historian W J Macqueen Pope ('Popie') told me, it was seen by seventy members of the cast during a rehearsal and, interestingly enough, it most frequently appears before or during the early days of a production. As such plays have invariably been successful the sighting of this theatre ghost has long been regarded as as good omen. The Man in Grey was seen just before the first night of *Oklahoma!* (1947), two days before *Carousel* opened (1950) and two days before *South Pacific* opened (1951); and he was seen within a few days of the opening nights of such successful musicals as *Glamorous Nights* (1935), *The Dancing Years* (1939), *The King and I* (1954) and *My Fair Lady* (1958), although he ignored *Pacific 1860* (1946) and other productions that turned out to be less than successful.

In common with most genuine spontaneous ghosts the Man in Grey makes no sound and walks in a preordained path, always moving in the same direction, counter-clockwise (withershins). Usually he is seen emerging out of the wall of a room on the left of the upper circle; he walks across that area, passing through some doors, turns left, ascends the stairs of the upper circle and walks right around the back and down the stairs on the other side, then through another door, and he disappears through a wall on the opposite side of the auditorium to that from which he appeared. Of course, often he is only seen briefly on part of his walk.

Most descriptions of the Man in Grey include powdered hair and a tricorn hat, riding boots and a long riding cloak over a dress jacket with ruffed sleeves, and he appears to carry a sword at his waist. No one has ever got nearer to him than about forty feet, but the many descriptions from witnesses are remarkably similar about his dress and his physical appearance: he has a strong face with a good chin, and is clean-shaven. Apart from theatre cleaners and staff, who have seen the ghost in the mornings while working, the Man in Grey has been reportedly seen by James Wentworth Day, the writer and ghost hunter; Stephen Williams, broadcasting officer for ENSA (Entertainments National Services Association), who took over the theatre during the Second World War; and by many actors and actresses – and, of course, by 'Popie', who told me he had seen the ghost several times.

The appearances of the Man in Grey are frequent, but not regular, and he appears to favour matinées and is never seen outside the daylight hours of 10.00 a.m. to 6.00 p.m.

There are many puzzling factors when we look at cyclic ghosts that seem to appear to date, irrespective of leap years or alterations in the calendar. But the fact remains that there is good evidence for some ghosts appearing only on certain days or at certain times, and there could be an important and crucial cyclic element to these happenings that we have not yet discovered.

A GHOST CALENDAR

JANUARY

19 Horses' hooves echo at Braddock Down, Cornwall, England, where Cromwell's army was defeated in 1643 during the English Civil War

FEBRUARY

12 A 'white shape' appears near the Bloody Tower at the Tower of London

13 Every fifty years a three-masted schooner, *Lady Luvibond*, sails off the Goodwin Sands on the Kent coast, where she sank in 1748

15 A drummer boy is seen on Hickling Broad, Norfolk, England
'Mrs Waggs' appears at Jenkyn Place in Hampshire on February afternoons

MARCH

17 'Juliet', who hanged herself near the Ferry Boat Inn in Cambridgeshire, England, appears there every year

APRIL

4 Lady Blanche de Warren haunts Rochester Castle, in Kent, England, where she was killed in 1264

9 An elderly lady in eighteenth-century clothes haunts Orme House on the Isle of Wight, off England's south coast

27 President Abraham Lincoln's funeral train travels from Washington DC to Illinois

MAY

1 The Irish hero O'Donoghue returns to Lough Leane, Co. Kerry, Ireland, at dawn; and the silent army of the Scottish hero Fingal appears on the shores of Loch Ashie near Inverness

17 A battle fought in 1828 during the Greek War of Independence is fought again near Frangocastello in Crete

19 A phantom coach drives towards Blickling Hall in Norfolk

31 Another coach, also in Norfolk, crashes into the old bridge at Potter Heigham

JUNE

4 A phantom sailor is seen in Ballyheigue Bay in Ireland

15 Hitchin Priory in Hertfordshire, England, is visited by a Civil War Cavalier who was killed nearby. On the same day, in America, but only every two years, a mysterious lady in pink appears in Yorba Family Cemetery in California

THE BLOODY Tower at the Tower of London, where a 'white shape' appears on 12 February each year

AN EXACT and unique model of Borley Rectory, long known as 'the most haunted house in England'

SIR WALTER Raleigh wished to be buried at Sherborne, but he lies at Westminster

JULY

5 Many strange sights are seen over the marshy fields in Somerset, England, where the Battle of Sedgemoor was fought in 1685

27 A red glow hangs over the Pass of Killicrankie, Scotland, scene of a bloody battle in 1689

28 The famous ghost nun walks the site of Borley Rectory in Essex, England

AUGUST

12 Six members of the Prussian Field Marshal Blücher's family reappear on the anniversary of his death

17· A ghost nun, Berta Rosata, haunts Chicksands Priory, Bedfordshire, England

Chicksands Priory –

SEPTEMBER

28 Sir Walter Raleigh returns to his old home, Sherborne Castle, England

A nineteenth-century guardsman, who was murdered one September in The Grenadier Inn at Hyde Park Corner, London, haunts there this month

Throughout this month strong feelings are experienced at Pacheco Pass in California, scene of many fights and atrocities over the years; and an unexplained Grey Man, associated with violent storms, haunts Pawley's Island off the East coast of America in the autumn

OCTOBER

23 Sounds of battle are heard, and soldiers seen, in Warwickshire at the site of the Battle of Edgehill, 1642

31 (Hallowe'en) Hauntings include: a soldier in Bournemouth (on England's south coast); a solitary monk at Minsden Chapel just north of London; a huntsman and his hound in Lancashire in the north of England; a phantom dog and chiming bells nearby at Armboth Fell in the Lake District; and six hooded figures at St Rita's in Chicago, USA

BRUCE CASTLE,
Tottenham, London, is
haunted by the screaming
Costania, who threw
herself to her death from
the balcony here after being
confined to one room by
her jealous husband, Lord
Coleraine, in the
seventeenth century. Every
3 November her screams
are reportedly heard again

NOVEMBER

1   Sir John Jocelyn rides down the drive of Hyde Hall in Hertfordshire, England, on his favourite white horse

3   Costania, Lady Coleraine, appears at Bruce Castle in north London, where she committed suicide

13   A 'grey lady' is seen at the Royal National Orthopaedic Hospital in Stanmore, north London

*c.*15   A monk haunts a church in Millvale, Pennsylvania, in the middle of this month, late at night

DECEMBER

Early in December a woman in black haunts the Stevenson House Museum in California; and at 'Christmas time' the ghostly children of William de Breose are seen at Bramber Castle, Sussex, England

21   All the ghosts in Britain meet at the Stiper Stones in Shropshire for the longest night of the year!

24   (Christmas Eve) Anne Boleyn walks at Hever Castle and Charles Dickens haunts Rochester Castle, both in Kent, England; a phantom monk wanders the ruins of Strata Florida Abbey in Wales and a sanctus bell tolls from the depths of Bomere Pool in Shropshire; while Roos Hall in Suffolk is visited by a coach and horses

24–5   The Queen of England's Norfolk residence, Sandringham, is also haunted at this time and, among other disturbances, Christmas cards are thrown to the floor

31   (New Year's Eve) Hauntings in England include King John's hounds in Dorset; a pig in Hampshire; a black horse in Norfolk; and a carriage which crosses the frozen Loch of Skene in Scotland. On the Isle of Wight the long-vanished house, Knighton Gorges, reappears at dusk – sometimes ablaze with lights and echoing music

LEFT: CHICKSANDS PRIORY
in Clophill, Bedfordshire,
England, was built between
1147 and 1153 and was
once the home of nuns of
the Gilbertine Order. It is
haunted by a ghost nun,
Berta Rosata, who has
frequently been seen and
heard on 17 August. The
property is now the centre
of RAF Chicksands and
houses the Officers' Club

BOTTOM LEFT: THE
GRENADIER at Hyde Park
Corner, London, was used
by officers of the Duke of
Wellington's Regiment
before Waterloo. A
nineteenth-century
guardsman haunts the
hostelry to this day

Ghosts

WHAT TO DO IF YOU SEE ONE

Millions of people believe they have seen ghosts, or witnessed ghostly activity or its results, or know someone who has seen a ghost. Although it is necessary to remember that our senses – sight, hearing, touch, even taste and smell – can all deceive us, it would appear that the evidence for ghosts, from different places and different people, is quite overwhelming and very convincing.

During psychical research it is always necessary, however, to keep one's feet firmly on the ground, and it is important to look thoroughly for a normal explanation before even thinking about a supernormal one. On most occasions, it has to be said, a normal explanation will be discovered: uncertain light; unfamiliar surroundings; and tiredness are just three common circumstances to be taken into account.

Strange noises can often be traced to faulty pipes, rodents, the wind or human interference. We have all heard sounds and seen sights we have not been able to explain, but just because we cannot find an explanation either immediately, or after careful exploration of all the circumstances, it does not mean that ghosts are responsible. There are such things as vibration and draughts, for example, and anything precariously balanced will, in all probability, eventually fall.

THE CASES THAT NEVER WERE

Any objective and experienced investigator will have stories to tell of happenings and occurrences that have almost deceived him. Sometimes these are conscious and involved, sometimes they are unconscious and simple misinterpretations of facts. Over the years I have come across many ghosts that are not ghosts, the faked, the false and the fraudulent. Sax Rohmer, creator of the Chinaman character, Fu Manchu, once wrote about a house found to be 'haunted' by mice with bells tied to their tails, who had been trained or enticed to run along the wainscot! I can't say I have ever encountered that particular deception but I have met hocus-pocus.

There was, for instance, what I have always (privately) called 'the case that never was'. Reports having been received of 'ghostly' music being heard repeatedly in a house in Sussex, I was asked by the Society for Psychical Research (SPR) in London to look into the case. They had sent two investigators to the house who had come back completely baffled. I made discreet enquiries and received a polite invitation to visit the house, where the owner-occupier told me many 'so-called experts' had visited him, and many of them had heard the music but could offer no explanation.

My first impression on meeting the owner, who lived by himself in the large house, was that he was a lonely man. He seemed to be completely relaxed and not at all troubled by the 'mysterious music' which, I was told, had been heard from all rooms on the ground floor of the house and at various times of the day and night. We sat in comfortable armchairs in a pleasant and light room, he in his favourite chair in the corner, I in the window alcove facing him. He talked at length about the music (which had never actually been identified) and of the people who had heard it. I asked all sorts of questions, and was told there were no special times, no cyclic element, no human presence that was conductive or obstructive, no legend or history or story associated with the house or its previous occupants that might account for the 'phantom music'.

After a while I thought I heard the faint sound of music, somewhat distant and seeming to originate in an adjoining room. I looked at my host. He returned my gaze with the ghost of a smile on his face. 'Yes, there it is – go and look if you like.' I went quietly into the next room, and the music stopped. He had followed me, and we went on a tour of the house. To cut a long story short, I spent the best part of three hours at the house. I noticed that the music was only heard to start when my host was sitting back in his chair so I subjected him to minute scrutiny and observed that his left hand moved, and seemed to clutch the padded armrest of his chair, just before the music started. Each time I let him think I was under the impression that the room where the music appeared to originate – sometimes one room, sometimes another, but always on the ground floor – was the important thing. But, in fact, I was watching him very carefully, and I noticed that whenever he left his chair the music stopped. Sometimes the music would be heard wherever I went if I wandered from room to room unattended, but never when he was by my side.

Eventually, when he disappeared into the kitchen with the tray of empty coffee-cups, I quickly examined his chair and discovered a series of small buttons hidden beneath the upholstery at the end of each armrest. I pressed one and immediately heard music! My host hurriedly returned and I resumed my seat on the other side of the room. He looked very annoyed, and this time *my* face bore the ghost of a smile. He knew the game was up and admitted that he was something of a gadget maniac and had fixed speakers and recorded music under the floorboards. He said he had had a lot of fun with people over six years, and he insisted that he had never said the music was 'ghostly' in origin: all his visitors had jumped to that conclusion.

'Well, do what you like,' he concluded. 'There will be no trace of anything here in twenty-four hours time. . .' We parted amicably and I never met him again, although several years later a researcher at the SPR asked me whether I had heard about a house on the south coast where the sound of a dog barking had been heard by members of the Society in an empty room – and had actually been recorded! Could I find a moment to look into the matter? When I heard the name of the occupant of the 'haunted' house, I didn't bother!

Tony Cornell, president of the Cambridge University Society for Psychical Research, once told me about a case that he looked into where a widower lived alone, the rest of the family having fled from the house 'because of a poltergeist'. After talking to the old man for some time – interrupted by the occasional 'bump' and 'bang' that seemed to have no cause or reason – Tony noticed that just prior to any of the noises the old fellow was quietly pulling on a piece of wire. He had rigged up his own ghost! It transpired that he had felt he was not wanted by his family, so he had driven them all out of the house.

John Cutten, one-time Secretary of the SPR, once said to me: 'Often what we are really doing is investigating the person rather than what they claim to see or experience. There are cases where it is possible to give a person a perfectly logical explanation, but they just will not accept it. This in itself is a most interesting study for there is no doubt that they believe sincerely that something supernormal has taken place.'

I once met a man who was convinced that ghosts were entities that could physically and psychologically inhabit human beings. When he was dying he told me, as I sat beside him, that he could feel a devil inside him – a devil who ran up and down inside his body – and that when it reached his heart he would die. Die he did, but I don't think it had anything to do with a little devil inside him. Perhaps we create our own devils and have to learn to live with them, or they may kill us.

FALSE GHOSTS

Many cases that have come to my attention have been the result of natural causes: patches of shadow; a branch tapping a window; light distorted through glass; moonlight reflecting off shiny, polished furniture or photographs or glazed pictures, giving the impression of a figure or an 'appearance' of some kind. Other people simply make mistakes.

A very sensible and down-to-earth lady wrote to me saying she had definitely seen a ghost, although she had never had any previous experience of the kind. She had passed in the street a friend she had known for years, a retired colonel, but next day she had read in the local newspaper that he had died the previous day, and she was convinced that she had seen his ghost. When I looked into the matter and saw the death certificate I discovered that she might indeed have seen her friend on the day she said, for he was alive and well at the time. He had suffered a heart attack and died a few hours after the time she gave for their meeting.

The twilight world between sleep and awaking is where many people think they see ghosts. But at such a time one's senses are not fully alert and working, so that a coat, hanging on a bedpost, can look just like a human figure; a passing car, its image distorted by the glass of a window pane and reflected in a mirror, can look like moving lights in the room; a bird that has fallen down a chimney and is flapping to find its way out can be taken for muffled footsteps climbing the stairs; an owl swooping silently past the window can become a 'white shape'; and a bat that has found its way into a room and flies about before escaping through an open window becomes a 'loud flapping of wings' very near at hand; and even a hat, left hurriedly in an unfamiliar place the evening before, can become a hooded figure in an uncertain light.

Some people see what they want to see and hear what they want to hear. Perhaps we should all think hard about what we see and decide in some instances whether we *want* to see what we think we hear. I always remember Walter de la Mare, the English writer and poet, telling me about the time he *almost* saw a ghost. He was staying in a reputedly haunted house and sleeping in the reputedly haunted room when, in 'the grey hours just before daylight', he found himself awake with the certain knowledge that there was a ghost in the room. He knew that he was fully conscious and awake, although he had not opened his eyes, and he lay there and reasoned with himself: if he turned his head and opened his eyes he would see the ghost; then, whatever happened next, he would not be able to get back to sleep for hours. Better not to look. He kept his eyes closed, and soon went back to sleep. Yet he told me he always regretted 'so abject a welcome' for someone who probably meant him no harm and who would, almost certainly, never visit him again – a ghost of memory and what might have been.

Even the famous story of the 'haunted' mummy-case in the British Museum in London may have been invented. It is supposed to have been cursed and to have brought bad luck and even death to various owners. Dr Margaret Murray was for years a member of the Ghost Club and she told me that she had invented the 'absurd' story of the haunted mummy-case on the spur of the moment when a fellow scientist, a great believer in the occult, begged her to tell the *real* story of the haunting. Margaret Murray couldn't resist the opportunity and proceeded to regale her gullible friend with a long and involved story which she was always amused to hear repeated by all sorts of people, as though it were the truth. When she took students to the British Museum to study Egyptian hieroglyphic writings she used to make a point of stopping outside the room containing the 'haunted' mummy-case and relating something of the legend. Then she would say that if any of her party believed such nonsense they need not face the cursed thing and they could stay where they were; and there were always some people in the party who waited outside the room.

ANOTHER HAUNTED chest is the Mistletoe Bough Chest at Bramshill, Hampshire in England, reputedly the chest where a bride hid. She became a famous ghost, seen by many responsible people, including a number of police officers who now occupy 'the most haunted house in Hampshire', which is a Police College

Then there is the story that Agatha Christie, the mystery writer, used to tell about the nineteenth-century inlaid chest she had found in Damascus. Writing at her riverside home in Devon in south-west England one night, she was astonished to hear what she described as 'ghostly munching' coming from the chest! After that first time she head the strange crumpling sound night after night, and eventually she took the chest to London to a firm of furniture restorers, who told her 'something sinister' seemed to be indicated. They spent three weeks investigating the problem and then asked her to call and collect the chest. When she did so she was shown 'a repulsive cross between a worm and a slug: it was large, white, obscene and obese beyond belief'. This imported monster had eaten a lot of the interior of the chest but the creature was disposed of, the chest was repaired and Agatha Christie had it in her possession for the rest of her life – without hearing another sound from it!

GENUINE CASES

Having examined a few examples of the possible explanations for reported psychic activity, what should the serious ghost hunter do when he has, to the best of his ability, eliminated all 'normal explanations'? There are several avenues open to the true seeker and more than one line of action that can be followed with impunity. There are those who feel that some ghosts are conscious entities who deserve help, which they are confident they can offer. We have had Ghost Club members who feel this way and on suitable occasions we give them every opportunity to do what they can. Personally I feel more in sympathy with those sharp-eyed but sympathetic investigators who try to think of ways to explain what has been observed but, having exhausted every normal explanation they can think of, accept that supernormal happenings do occur.

So what should you do if you really think you see a ghost? For many years the Ghost Club of Great Britain has given enquirers a short answer: stand still and observe as much as you can. If the figure disappears through a doorway or behind a wall, follow quietly. Carefully note the time, and other details, and see whether anyone else has had a similar experience – and if they have, obtain corroborative evidence.

The fullest account of any apparently paranormal experience should be written down as soon as possible after the event, together with supporting accounts from any other witnesses. Many investigators feel that the longer a person waits before reporting what has been seen or heard, the more likely it is to be exaggerated. The police take a similar view of reported incidents. As one American investigator has put it: 'the greater the wait, the bigger the whopper'. With the passing of a few days, even a few hours, a strange light becomes a blinding flash, a squeaky stair becomes heavy footsteps and a falling object becomes a thunderous bang and so on.

Here are a few dos and don'ts that are really common sense, but well worth bearing in mind when you visit a haunted house or talk to someone about their experiences.

DON'T be frightened. So-called ghosts, including poltergeists, rarely, if ever, hurt anyone. Certain sounds and sights may be startling and there may be damage to furniture and rooms, but it is unlikely that anyone has been injured. The human eye has often been found to be a deterrent in the case of poltergeist activity with articles in flight suddenly dropping to the ground.

It may also be that apparitions, spectres, phantoms, call them what you will, are in a different dimension from human beings. This could be why spontaneous ghosts rarely, if ever, seem to be aware of the presence of human beings and why they often seem to appear in the same place and do the same thing, be it walking or gliding along a passage or a path or manifesting briefly in one particular room. Evidence suggests that many spontaneous ghosts appear and disappear whether or not a human being is present.

DO investigate immediately and write a report promptly. For example, if an object moves, draw a sketch of its path and note its weight. Most poltergeist-projected objects finish up at a lower level than where they were originally, thereby using the minimum amount of energy. Explore the possibility that a thread or wire could have been loosely attached to the object, or that it could have been projected in some other way by normal means. Search carefully for any signs of cotton, paste, chewing-gum or anything similar that might hold an object for a limited time.

Be sure you know the position of everyone in the house or vicinity at the time an incident occurs and obtain signed and dated notes from them all.

Do try to take a photograph of the effect, of a ghost, of the people who are witnesses and, indeed, of anything that pertains to the case. Such photographs can be of considerable value in enabling other people to visualize what has happened, and where, and to whom, perhaps helping them suggest a normal explanation that had not occurred to you.

DON'T publicize the case or talk about it without the express permission of the people concerned. Families are often highly embarrassed and even frightened by newspaper, radio and television reporters. There have been many instances where thoughtless words have brought hordes of people to a reportedly haunted house and eventually, in an effort to stop the unwelcome attention, the occupants have said that nothing really happened and they were mistaken all the time. In other cases the investigator is shown the door in no uncertain manner, and I know of one otherwise good reporter of apparently paranormal activity who has allowed his love of personal publicity to get the better of him so that he has been forced to give up all association with several cases.

Once you have broken a confidence you will not be trusted again so learn to talk about a case, or to publicise the story of an investigation, only after it is completed and once you have obtained the permission of the relevant people. Careful attention to this aspect of ghost hunting will pay dividends, many times over.

Do obtain help, if you feel it is needed, with the permission of the people concerned. Go to a doctor, a churchman, a friend of the family or anyone else who can be trusted. Don't forget that organizations such as the Ghost Club or the College of Psychic Studies (see p.120) have experienced people at their beck and call, together with access to useful apparatus that can perhaps establish scientifically that what is reported is not a figment of the imagination or the result of wishful thinking or poor observation.

(Incidentally, a simple but effective way of establishing to your own satisfaction that what you are seeing is objective and not subjective, is to lightly depress one eye, disturbing your vision. If the 'ghost' is distorted, then what you are seeing is indeed objective; if the 'ghost' remain clear and undistorted, then what you are seeing is in your mind only.)

It should be realised and accepted that there is nothing credulous or gullible about someone investigating haunted houses and similar phenomena. Either such phenomena do occur, or they do not, and either way it is the task of the psychic investigator to study and record such happenings, or lack of them, in a perfectly calm, cool and judicial manner.

But it cannot be emphasised too much that attempts should be made to obtain permanent records of any visual or auditory phenomena, and to observe what happens in a purely scientific spirit. Every possible normal hypothesis must be considered with the utmost care before

BURFORD PRIORY, Oxfordshire, England, has long been haunted by a little brown monk and the sound of a tolling bell. The ghost has been seen in various parts of the Priory and grounds, often walking through walls and other solid objects. The sound of chanting monks has been reported close to the old Priory burial ground

looking for a possible paranormal explanation. Occasionally fraud *will* be unearthed; lying; practical jokes; trickery. Often *normal* causes will be discovered: the wind; hot water pipes; bats; rats; vibration. Fear, suggestion, expectancy or hallucination may each play their part, too, and must be taken into account.

DON'T be put off by the thought that you need costly or complicated equipment. The presence of ghostly activity, or at any rate unexplained activity, can sometimes be established by simple methods. (See p. 110 for some advice on ghost hunting equipment.) During a Ghost Club investigation, following the production of a puzzling photograph which appeared to represent a figure with its hand on the iron rail of a staircase (taken by a clergyman and his wife in seemingly impeccable circumstances), we smeared a little petroleum jelly on the handrail, hoping for the handprint of a ghost, but we were unlucky! Talcum powder or flour is often used in a room or passage where disembodied footfalls have been heard – or sugar, which enhances the sound of footsteps but which ghosts seem to be wary of, or to treat with aversion. There was an instance of a shop where the assistants

ST MICHAEL'S Mount in Cornwall dates from the fourteenth century. A few years ago Lord St Levan told me that he possessed a seventeenth-century four-poster bed with such a curious and terrifying atmosphere that no child was able to spend a night in the bed. Other reported disturbances include a mysterious and ghostly White Lady

repeatedly asserted they heard light footsteps on a deserted stairway and in one particular (deserted) room. The floor of this unused room was sprinkled with talcum powder and it was sealed. Small footprints were apparently discovered when the room was opened next morning – but for some inexplicable reason the footprints were not photographed, nor were signed and witnessed statements obtained.

One well-established scientific aspect of a haunting is a drop in temperature, which has also been noticed on many occasions at spiritualistic seances when psychic activity has been reported. There is overwhelming evidence that the temperature does drop just before and during ghostly activity.

I recall an investigation where a ghost monk was reported to walk along a track now partly occupied by a pigsty and horse stabling. We placed thermometers in the pigsty, in the stables and in other nearby positions and they were all regularly checked throughout the night. None of them showed any abnormality until just after 2.00 a.m., when we were surprised to hear the sound of the pigs suddenly fighting for a moment, followed by the whinnying and pawing of the horses. We discovered the temperature in the pigsty and in the stables had suddenly and inexplicably dropped seven degrees. Elsewhere the temperature was normal, and ten minutes later these two thermometers registered no abnormality either. It is well known that animals, especially horses, are psychically aware and it may be that some ghostly remnant passed through the pigsty and stables that night, on the old monks' track.

Every ghost hunter will have tales to tell of hours and hours spent in cold and draughty rooms and corridors waiting for ghosts that did not appear – for if there is one certainty about ghosts it is their unpredictability, and even should they appear it is likely that they will only be visible to one or two people among the watchers.

However, should you be lucky (or unlucky) enough to encounter a ghost, Harry Price, ghost hunter extraordinary during the 1920s and 1930s, produced a form of conduct that cannot be bettered: 'Do not move, and on no account approach the figure,' he said in his famous *Blue Book of Instructions*. 'If the figure speaks, *do not approach,* but ascertain name, age, sex, origin, cause of visit, if in trouble, and possible alleviation. Ask the figure to return, suggesting exact time and place. Do not move until figure disappears. Note exact method of vanishing. If through an open doorway, quietly follow. If through a solid object (such as a wall) ascertain if still visible on the other side.'

There is very little evidence of spontaneous ghosts speaking, but the advice is good, especially when you remember that Price was breaking new ground, and it is difficult to argue with his counsel.

To sum up: any time you think you can see a ghost keep your wits about you; look for a 'normal' explanation; observe everything you can; write a full report of the incident as soon as possible; and then get in touch with me!

Ghosts

PRACTICAL AIDS FOR THE GHOST HUNTER

I have always believed that simple and uncluttered investigation of a haunted house is just as valuable as the most elaborate and sophisticated investigation. However, proof is enhanced by demonstrable records: photographs and sound recordings, for example, and, of course, the evidence of other witnesses.

Your first requirement, and one that costs nothing at all, is to train yourself to be observant at all times: if you notice a movement anywhere at any time seek to discover what caused it; if you enter a room and see something out of place, or something missing, make a point of establishing that your observation was correct. Training yourself in this way will pay dividends when you come to ghost hunting, when every movement of every object may be of the greatest value in an investigation.

PART OF the Ghost Club's ghost-hunting equipment

EQUIPMENT

A bag, box or case for the easy transportation of the ghost hunter's equipment, and somewhere to store such equipment, must be regarded as more or less essential. But it is not worth spending too much on a bag until you are completely happy with the equipment you have collected. The various items can soon take up a lot of room and it is a good idea to collect the essentials, or what you feel you can afford and are comfortable with, first. There are some very useful collapsible bags around these days, although you might prefer a solid suitcase or something of that sort. Anything with partitions can make a useful container for the smaller essentials, with perhaps another bag or case for the less essential but 'useful-on-occasions' articles.

A notebook is your first essential and the ones stationery shops sell for reporters are ideal. It is imperative to have all reports, and even your notes, carefully detailed as to the time and place they were made. This will eliminate countless problems later on, so get into the habit of *always* putting the date and place before you start.

You can make your notes in ballpoint pen or pencil; pen is more durable but always ensure you have a spare one as they invariably run out at the most inconvenient moment. Pencils should be sharpened before each prospective investigation (but take a sharpener), and a few coloured pencils or crayons are useful for clear and precise plans and rough on-the-spot maps. They can also be useful for assistant ghost hunters; if each one uses a different colour there can be no confusion as to who made a particular note or sketch-map. A small soft pencil eraser should also be readily available.

Take a few sheets of plain paper, for sketches, plans etc., and if they are cut to the same size as the notebook they can be kept neatly at the back, ready for immediate use.

A VISITOR to the old Angel Hotel, Guildford, England, saw the ghost of a man in late eighteenth-century military uniform reflected in the mirror of his bedroom wardrobe. The ghost was seen by two people for more than twenty minutes and one witness hurriedly drew what he saw using a blue ball-point pen and a red paper napkin (above)

Sticks of chalk and artists' willow charcoal are useful for marking walls and furniture and have the advantage of being easily rubbed off. The latter shows up less well than the former but is not always apposite – if it is to be used on dark furniture, for instance.

Another inexpensive item is a reel of black synthetic thread, and perhaps one each of black and white cotton thread. The synthetic thread is to stretch across stairways, corridors, passages and doorways; it will not break easily, and if a human being attempts a noiseless entry the resulting sounds are likely to be heard in the quiet ghost-watching hours. The cotton, on the other hand, is for use in similar places which are under observation, or are the subject of investigation with thermometers or triggered photography – the idea being that whatever breaks the cotton will not notice and the event will be recorded.

Similarly, thin fuse wire can be used which, when broken, will break an electric circuit and alert the watchers. Strong gardening twine or something similar is useful to tie up a door or cupboard handle, secure a window latch or prevent entry via the chimney. Electric cord, thick nylon twine, even rolls of bandages, can be used for the same purposes. Wool (black, white and brown) can be used for controlling articles under observation: it will break if an object moves. Surgical adhesive tape and opaque black or coloured adhesive tape are useful for the same reason for making permanent seals – which can also be achieved by using lead seals and sealing wax. Gummed paper, transparent or white, can also have its use, as can gummed red and gold stars and a few tie-on luggage labels for identification or information purposes.

A camera, or cameras, should always accompany the ghost hunter on any investigation. Colour, black-and-white and infra-red films have all been used with interesting results and as there are schools of thought that claim each type of film is more sensitive to ghostly activity, take all three in three different cameras if you can.

The actual camera, or cameras, to use must be dictated by your personal preference or financial considerations, but get as good a one as possible, with a tripod. A simple and inexpensive camera is all that is really necessary – and the fewer the controls the more chance there is of obtaining a photograph of something in the event of a sudden movement or unexpected appearance. But, of course, a better result will usually be obtained with more sophisticated equipment and there is a lot to be said for the Polaroid type. The fully-automatic cameras that are now available also have many advantages because they take photographs instantly. The use of a cine camera can also be of considerable assistance, particularly where the area to be controlled is extensive, or in poltergeist cases.

Always remember to take spare black-and-white (fast) and colour films, batteries and flash bulbs; and also infra-red films and additional lenses, filters, shades and various automatic attachments and other refinements according to taste, experience and the finance available.

While the question of whether or not ghosts can be photographed is still open to question, there are a number of photographs that seem to be genuine and appear to depict a form or figure that may or may not have been seen by the photographer (see p.61). So it is always worth taking photographs whenever the temperature drops; whenever anyone has the feeling that something is about to happen; whenever a person who has seen the ghost returns to the spot; or, indeed, whenever you feel it might be worth taking a photograph. You never know, *something* may appear on the film. Always keep a careful note of the date, time and place where each photograph is taken. Sometimes photographs will reveal fraud and it is very important to know when and how deception is being practised.

A detailed record of the haunted room, house, garden, yard or whatever is an important aspect of any investigation, and to enable such plans to be prepared it is necessary to include in your ghost-hunting kit measures of various kinds: tape measures, both a simple dressmaker's yard measure and an architect's 33-foot leather-cased winding tape, or something of the sort, are especially useful; as are steel measures and wooden or metal rulers. You might also take a spring balance for measuring the weight of an article allegedly moved by paranormal means; and a strain gauge for measuring the force necessary to close or open a door, drawer or cupboard.

Other odds and ends that will be found to be useful on occasion include: impact adhesive; rubber bands; an assortment of small screws and screw-eyes; nails of various sizes; tintacks; drawing pins; and colour-headed pins. You should also include: a small hammer; a screwdriver or two; a bradawl; some pliers; some wire-clippers; and a plumb-line.

Transparent envelopes and containers for questionable and dubious substances are useful for preserving such matter until it can be examined and identified. A careful note of exactly when and where the substance was found should be attached to the sample. Also, take talcum powder, flour or sugar to sprinkle for footprints or fingerprints.

I have found luminous card and paper very useful, both for marking objects and places and as directional indicators. You will also need a pair of stout scissors, a pen-knife and several magnifying glasses (I have a small hand magnifier, a large quality specimen and a watchmaker's loupe that can be held in the eye). Nor should you forget a pair of tennis shoes, or something similar, for comfort, cleanliness in a stranger's house and to enable you to walk about without being heard. A reliable torch – with batteries – is a must.

A dependable watch is essential, and one with a luminous or illustrated dial is preferable. In addition to ensuring that each member of my investigating team has a watch – and all watches are synchronized at the commencement of each ghost hunt – I also put a simple quartz clock on a table in the base room (the room where

THE HAUNTED Priest Room at Chingle Hall, Lancashire, in England, where many psychic manifestations have been reported, including a ghostly monk-like figure and loud vibrating crashing sounds that were, nevertheless, confined to the small room. However, sound recording apparatus set up just outside the room recorded nothing. Several exorcisms have failed to eradicate the ghost activity here

operations are planned, reports made and rotas decided). A stop watch is also useful.

The more ingenious ghost hunter might like to make simple gadgets at the scene of a haunting and for this purpose dry batteries, switches, small electric bells, light bulbs and bulb-holders, together with supplies of various grades of wire, will be needed. A coil of heavy-duty electric cable and an assortment of electric plugs and adapters might be included, and a voltmeter for checking electrical power faults.

Thermometers are also essential ghost-hunting tools. A good supply of the simple and inexpensive ones, suitable for indoor or outdoor use, must be part of your equipment. Check them at regular intervals when they are in place during an investigation. (This is a chore that can be arranged on a rota basis, and it can be linked with other routine checking and patrolling of the allegedly haunted areas.) In addition to the simple everyday thermometers, several other types are useful to the ghost hunter. The eighteen-inch or greenhouse models register prominently any sudden fluctuation in temperature, which can easily be spotted. The maximum-and-minimum thermometers are useful for positioning in inaccessible places, such as beside a chimney stack or outside an upstairs window, and they will show the highest and lowest temperatures recorded over any given period. The self-registering thermographs are an even greater help for they automatically record a graph showing the temperature wherever they are sited. Whatever type, or types, of thermometers are used, do number them and keep a clear and careful record of each, detailing where it was positioned, when and for how long.

Other apparatus of considerable help in investigations includes: portable and static sound recorders (especially the sensitive ones that

THIS GHOSTLY image appeared on a time-exposure film of Limassol Bay, Cyprus

can be left outside a room to record any sound within it); frequency change detectors; instruments for measuring atmospheric pressure, vibration, wind force and humidity. Other appliances, such as metal-detectors, walkie-talkie sets, sound scanners, magnetometers and electric field measuring devices add to the scientific record of a haunting (and might help to ease the boredom of a quiet night). But they do add considerable weight and expense to your kit. If neither is a consideration, then you can explore the possible use of even more sophisticated alarm and detection equipment, closed-circuit television, video cameras, capacity-change recorders, infra-red telescopes, thermal-heat scanners, anemometers, ventimeters and air meters.

I knew one ghost hunter who took over five tons of equipment with him, and another who had a van permanently loaded with every type of ghost-hunting equipment you can imagine. (But I have to say that the reports from both these quarters were of no more interest to the scientist, or anyone else, than those prepared by an amateur with the simplest and most straightforward ghost-hunting apparatus.)

A large-scale map of the area concerned is always very useful, and a compass. I have also found a Milograph map measure extremely helpful. Take one or two mirrors placed in strategic positions: these have often told me a great deal in a short time about what is happening out of sight. For years I have used an old car wing-mirror that swivels in all directions.

I have also found it useful to have with me a number of possibly evocative articles that can be left in various positions, carefully ringed with chalk, and checked regularly. Sometimes the 'ghost' will be that of a child and toys will be an attraction; often a murder has been committed so an appropriate weapon might be useful; sometimes religion has a bearing on the case, so I usually take suitable symbols with me, such as a small bell, a doll, a ball, a paper-knife, a dagger, a bible, a crucifix or a photograph. On occasion such miscellanea will apparently help to promote phenomena and, in any case, they provide interest for everyone present and can lighten the atmosphere. Try Zener Cards, with symbols of a cross, circle, square, star and wavy lines; and word-association tests, to explore the possible extra-sensory perception (ESP) of the nexus of the poltergeist and other occupants of the affected house; while I have often found both routine and specially-compiled intelligence tests and similar experiments to be both interesting and revealing. These show the way people's minds work, and how they judge disturbances or react to them.

WHERE TO HUNT

The physical features near a haunted house are frequently the focal point of supernormal power. Such features might be a pool, a wood, crossroads, a quarry, even a tree. It is, therefore, always worth concentrating part of a night at a haunted location to discovering such a focal point and then seeing whether you or any of your companions experience any feelings at that spot, and whether any of the available apparatus shows any abnormality – and frequently it does.

There are often certain parts of a house, or things in it, that can attract ghosts. The most haunted part of a house is frequently the staircase, so it could be advisable to spend a lot of time in the vicinity of the staircase in a reputedly haunted house. Other parts of a house that are often found to be more haunted than the rest include the cellars and the cellar steps. Pay attention to reputedly haunted pieces of furniture, too. It is possible that any second-hand furniture that seems to attract ghosts may have come from haunted houses.

I think there is no argument but that simple ghost hunting equipment is just as effective in the investigation of ghostly activity as the most sophisticated of apparatus. The value of any report is really only as good as the investigators concerned and it is never entirely dependent upon the equipment used. It is most important, therefore, that the integrity, honesty, sincerity and accuracy of the ghost hunter is never brought into question. But human nature being what it is, once you are a successful ghost hunter there are sure to be some people who seek to disparage your efforts. Strive, therefore, to be straightforward, kind and understanding, but above all be truthful at all times.

THE STAIRCASE is often the most haunted part of a house. The ghost of Mary Queen of Scots walks down the staircase at the Talbot Hotel, Oundle in Northamptonshire, where she walked just before her execution. There is a crown-shaped mark on the baluster which is supposed to have been made by the Queen's ring

THE GHOST of an Edwardian lady walks up the silver stairway at Manderston House in Duns, a mansion owned by Lord Palmer of the Huntley & Palmer biscuit family, and known as 'Scotland's Versailles'. She is thought to be the wife of Sir James Palmer, the second baronet

Ghosts

A PROBLEM FOR SCIENCE

There seems to be a striking paradox in psychical research, for science today, by its own laws, is being forced towards what would, up to now, have been regarded as an unscientific attitude. Every scientist worthy of the name has to admit that the world is a far more complicated place that it was once thought to be, and almost daily the scientific world edges towards accepting psychical research as a science.

Some scientists and scientifically-minded people will say, somewhat vaguely, that psychical research is all 'mind phenomena'. Unfortunately the term 'mind' is a very loosely defined concept. We know well enough what a person means when he tells us that his mind is confused, or that so-and-so has a brilliant mind, or that someone else's mind has become deranged; but in each of these examples the word 'brain' might easily be substituted for the word 'mind'. To philosophers, the term 'mind' is used to cover an enormous variety of meanings. The psychologists have further muddied the water by attributing to the mind semi-mechanical qualities, while theologians equate the mind with the ancient idea of the soul. Some psychical researchers seek to reap the benefit of this confusion by using any or all of these views on the nature of the mind, not hesitating to add to them or subtract from them, as it suits them.

The fallacy is to regard the mind as a separate entity, a thing in itself, when all it really means is the brain in action. 'Mental processes' 'mental activity' and similar terms have replaced the word 'mind' in modern psychiatry. The mind, as such, does not exist; it possesses no scientific definition – what we are really dealing with is the result of the brain in action.

It has long been accepted that scholars and scientists make poor psychical researchers or ghost hunters. They are usually too used to working in an atmosphere of trust and intellectual objectivity and they are seldom equipped for a task that requires the training of a psychologist, the flair of a detective and the experience of a conjuror.

Physicists might do well to explore the possibility that there exists a psychic force, a continuum of power, all pervasive and powerful, that can cause 'stresses' to occur which so concentrate the psychic force that it has the equivalent of 'solidity' of matter. In other words a haunted house or locality may represent a 'thickening' in the fields of psychic force in the same way as 'matter' may be a thickening or joining of the space-time concept.

Professor H Habberley Price, FBA, Wykeham Professor of Logic at Oxford University, told me that if he were asked the age-old question 'Do you believe in ghosts?' he would reply that it was first necessary to define what a ghost is. His definition was: 'a visible but non-physical entity closely resembling a physical human being either living or dead'. And he was fond of referring to two very different yet similar cases. One was the appearance of an airman shot down over France during the First World War, apparently seen in India by his half-sister. In this case the distance between the physical human being and the non-physical entity was very great. But this distance may be small and, indeed, both may be seen at the same time, as in the second case of a lady seated at her dining table with three other people. They all saw an apparition of their hostess only a few feet away and she saw it too.

On the available evidence, these non-physical entities, claimed Professor Price, may be audible as well as visible, and some were only audible to some people and only visible to others. It was particularly interesting to note that when an entity resembling a human being was the central figure of the apparition, this figure usually had appurtenances or accompaniments which were equally apparitional, such as the clothes the figure wore, the carriage it might be in, or anything the figure might be carrying.

Crisis cases, probably the best documented cases of apparitional appearances, have led some researchers, such as G N M Tyrrell, to favour a telepathic theory for many apparitions. Interestingly enough it is fairly well established that the process of telepathy is a two-stage process. In the first place the telepathic impression is received at some unconscious level of the perceiver's mind, and in the second place that impression manifests itself to the consciousness. But it seems that some impressions simply don't emerge into consciousness, or only emerge imperfectly or in part.

My old friend Professor Price believed that the second stage could emerge in different forms: as a dream; as a waking mental image; in a crystal ball, or something of the sort; in the form of a hunch (an unreasoned belief which turns out to be correct); or as an unreasoned impulse to do or say something; occasionally, too, in forms of automatic or semi-automatic behaviour such as automatic writing or speech. If this theory were correct, apparitions would be the most complete and most dramatic method and manifestation of a telepathic impression. 'If we have telepathic dreams,' Professor Price said to me on several occasions, 'why not telepathic hallucinations? Since they are similar phenomena, we might well call dreams hallucinations in sleep and hallucinations waking dreams.'

The great difficulty with the telepathic theory has always been how it can be considered in relation to collective cases – that is, apparitions seen or heard by several people. Cats, dogs and horses often appear to see such 'public hallucinations', too, which further complicates matters.

Professor Price and other experienced investigators have always recognized that there is considerable evidence for objective entities which are not purely hallucinatory – an experience independent of the mind and brain seeing it. These images appear to pass through matter, through closed doors, walls and so forth; they look solid but seem to operate within the laws of psychology. They are images made visible to other people and this leads to the suggestion that they are something between the mental and the physical, not quite belonging to either. Both these theories, according to Professor Price, were useful in making some sense of phenomena that appeared to have no reality or reason.

Temperature is a measure of the rate at which heat is transferred to or from a body or building, a measure of the kinetic energy of the molecules or atoms of which matter is composed. Under certain conditions a space may be created, called a vacuum, in which there are no molecules or atoms. Scientists tell us that a perfect vacuum is unobtainable since all material surrounding a space has a vapour pressure, so the term vacuum is generally taken to mean a space containing air at very low pressure. When a ghost is present it seems to create a partial vacuum, with a resulting drop in pressure and temperature variation which is measured by a thermometer – either a simple one or a thermograph, which registers the temperature by itself on a graph. How a ghost can do this is a mystery not yet solved by scientists.

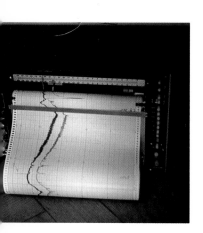

CONSTANT TEMPERATURE recordings made during the investigation of a poltergeist case in Mulhouse, France, showed inexplicable temperature fluctuations

Professor A C Hardy of Oxford University, a well-known zoologist, declared in 1949, to the British Association for the Advancement of Science, his belief that the existence of telepathy had been scientifically demonstrated. He reminded his fellow scientists that 'the communication of one mind to another by means other than by the ordinary senses' might well alter our ideas on evolution and psychical phenomena – perhaps the most important of all areas of study for mankind.

One present-day scientist and astro-physicist, Dr Percy Seymour of Plymouth University, in Devon, has published and endorsed the theory that all matter in the universe leaves an indelible trace in the form of a so-called 'worldline', rather like a wake left by a ship, showing where it has been. These permanent tracks of energy are the answer to the mystery of ghosts, says Dr Seymour. 'We all leave our footprints on the sands of time. As we move about, as we create our personalities within the constraints imposed on us by our genetic inheritance, as we establish our own patterns of behaviour and we turn some of these patterns into habits, so we are leaving our footprints in the sands of time. . . A person of firm and strong habits who has lived at the same place for a very long time would leave a strong "imprint" on the world-lines passing through that place. . . and it may be possible for anyone to tune into that image.'

For a scientist to suggest or admit the possibility that there is an acceptable explanation for the paranormal, and that a so-called haunted house need not involve life after death, that ghosts are not only possible but real and explicable by science, is a giant step for the scientific world to take.

Dr Seymour says his work draws on ideas gaining ground with a growing number of scientists trying to understand the sub-atomic world, a debate that goes back to the 1920s between Albert Einstein and other physicists over the rules that govern atoms – Einstein being unable to accept that it is impossible to know everything about a sub-atomic particle at any given time.

He could not accept the 1927 discovery, known as the Uncertainty Principle, which later became a corner-stone of modern physics. This said that in everything there is an uncertain element that has to be allowed for. But since 1950 a number of eminent physicists have felt that the principle is little more than a symptom of our ignorance. They point out that if we could somehow see 'beneath' observed reality, it could well become clear that sub-atomic particles are in fact being jostled by 'unseen forces'; and if this jostling is taken into account it would be possible to eliminate the uncertainty that Einstein found impossible to accept.

Dr Seymour, seeking to explain the interconnection of sub-atomic phenomena, which could well open the door to an explanation of several aspects of the paranormal, calls the unseen world in which these forces operate 'plasma space'. His theory has yet to receive approval from the scientific world, but it is clear that the area he seeks to investigate is a level of space inaccessible to the senses and to scientific instruments – and therefore beyond our present understanding of reality. It is most certainly a step in the right direction.

BALLINDALLOCH CASTLE, Grampians, Scotland, is a sixteenth-century tower linked to a modern building and is haunted by a ghostly Green Lady who brings misfortune to those who meet her. She is thought to have been an owner or occupant of the castle 200 years ago, who died after being jilted. Appearances and disturbances are less frequent than they were, except in the vicinity of the old tower

Ghosts

USEFUL ORGANIZATIONS
AND BOOKS WORLDWIDE

A great deal of help and information is available to the enthusiastic ghost hunter who is not afraid to seek it out. Apart from books (see p.127), the Reference Departments of local libraries are mines of information, and the librarians are usually very helpful and extremely knowledgeable about local places, properties and people.

GREAT BRITAIN

Local spiritualist organizations can also provide information that you might not otherwise have expected to discover; they invariably seem to have at least one member who is aware of local stories of hauntings and, in all probability, can supply you with information concerning the haunting you are investigating in the area.

The Spiritualist Association of Great Britain
33 Belgrave Square
London SW1X 8QL

The Spiritualist National Union
Redwoods, Stansted Hall
Stansted, Essex CM24 8UD

These two international organizations together run about 2,250 spiritualist churches in Britain alone, with an estimated 90,000 active members, and they are invariably helpful.

The Greater World Christian Spiritualist Association
3 Conway Street
London W1P 5HA

This has about 150 affiliated churches and practises traditional Christian beliefs alongside spiritualism.

Psychic News
2 Tavistock Chambers, Bloomsbury Way
London WC1A 2SE

This is the spiritualist weekly newspaper, which often mentions current reports of hauntings, usually without going into great detail. Enquiries at the London office are dealt with promptly and willingly. *Psychic News* issues a Yearbook and Catalogue, which contains addresses of spiritualist centres throughout the world and other information of special interest to spiritualists.

Two Worlds

67 Plumstead High Street
London SE18 1SB

This is also a spiritualist magazine, which dates from 1887.

Membership of a responsible organization devoted to the study of the paranormal is likely to be helpful on several levels. Most hold meetings where subjects of interest to the ghost hunter are discussed, and often there are lectures and talks by experienced researchers and investigators. Some of the societies have excellent libraries where it is possible to consult the best books on the subject. There are always helpful society members, too, who are ready and willing to share their experiences and knowledge with new members. A few of these organizations have facilities for ghost-hunting investigations in which members may be able to participate, learning at first-hand the best methods to employ and the standards to aspire to – and the atmosphere to be encountered in a genuine haunted house – all in the company of experienced ghost hunters.

Here are a few of the societies and organizations likely to be of help and interest to the sincere ghost hunter.

The Ghost Club

c/o Peter Underwood, The Savage Club
1 Whitehall Place
London SW1A 2HD

Founded in 1862, it is the oldest and most respected of British investigating organizations, with a wealth of experienced and friendly members, unrivalled facilities, and opportunities for participating in haunted house investigations. Membership is normally by invitation only, but for further details write direct.

The College of Psychic Studies

16 Queensberry Place
London SW7 2EB

It has changed its name several times, but has always been highly regarded for its sincerity and integrity. It has an excellent library, publishes a magazine *Light*, three times a year, conducts healing, meditation, psychic and development courses and has a very full programme of lectures, workshops and classes. There are also opportunities for private interviews with 'sensitives' and for training in mediumship. The college is open to anyone interested in the paranormal and has three categories of membership: Associate, Full Member and Fellow.

The Unitarian Society for Psychical Studies
c/o Rev. Vernon Marshall, 7 Greenhill Road
Moseley, Birmingham B13 9SR

Founded in 1965, this is a religion-based society. It issues periodical Journals and holds an annual conference – as well as other meetings – usually in Birmingham. The quality of the talks and discussions is high and the articles, letters and contributions to the Journal are often significant and helpful. The aim of the society is to 'encourage the study of psychical phenomena in all aspects, with a critical and open mind'.

The Association for the Scientific Study of Anomalous Phenomena (ASSAP)
c/o David Christie-Murray
Imber Court Cottage, Orchard Lane
East Molesey, Surrey KT8 0BN

This was founded in 1981 and seeks to investigate paranormal activity in its widest sense – including such twentieth-century phenomena as UFOs, metal bending and crop circles. Its approach is scientific and its publications include a Newsletter, the journal *Anomaly* and occasional papers, books and booklets. Details of ASSAP can be obtained by writing direct.

The London Society for Psychical Research
49 Marloes Road
London W8 6LA

This was founded in 1882 by a group of spiritualists, but it has recently become less respected as there has been quarrelling between members about things that happened decades ago and its articles are very long, almost unreadable and statistically-orientated. Anyone can join.

The British Unidentified Flying Object Research Association (BUFORA)
c/o John Spencer, Suite 1, 2c Layton Road
Harpenden, Herts AL5 2TL

Founded in 1964, this organization investigates all aspects of UFO exploration, including relevant ghosts and apparitions and their possible correlation. The society conducts scientific research, issues a bi-monthly *UFO Times* and holds meetings in London. Membership is open to sympathetic applicants who are approved by the society's council. Write for details.

The Noah's Ark Society
c/o Alan Crossley, Street Farm House
Scole, Diss, Norfolk 1121 4DR

This will be of interest to people intrigued by the induced phenomena of the seance room as much as by spontaneous ghosts and hauntings. Established in 1990, there are now about 400 members throughout the country, comprising circles of seven or eight people each. They hold seances for the development of 'physical' phenomena. The President organizes and runs the society, arranging occasional residential seminars and other activities for members. While the majority of the members have come to the organization via spiritualism, many of them feel the emphasis within the circles is, and should be, primarily on the phenomena themselves.

Strange Phenomena Investigations (SPI)
41 The Braes, Tullibody
Alloa, Scotland FK10 2TT

Scottish UFO Research (SRUFO)
14 Relupas Gardens
Edinburgh, Scotland EH9 2PU

Centre for Crop Circle Studies (CCCS)
20 Paul Street
Frome, Somerset BA11 1DX

Institute of Psychophysical Research
118 Banbury Road
Oxford OX2 6JU

Paraphysical Study Group
International Parascience Institute
Cryndir, Nantmel
Llandrindod Wells, Powys LD1 6EH

The Theosophical Society
50 Gloucester Place
London W1H 3HJ

The British Society of Dowsers
Sycamore Cottage, Tamley Lane
Hastingleigh, Ashford
Kent TN25 5HW

Society of Metaphysicians (Metaphysical Research Group)
Archers Court, Stonestile Lane
Hastings, Sussex TN35 4PG

Ghostbusters UK
c/o Robin Furman, 4 Weelsby Road
Grimsby, South Humberside DN32 0PP

Their equipment includes an Acorn computer that can monitor changes in temperature, light and vibration, and is attached to sound-recording equipment. They transport themselves in a 'Ghostmobile' and their aim is to build up a sufficient number of print-outs of different types of paranormal activity to be able to locate patterns that could be invaluable in the study of psychic activity.

United States of America and Canada

The American Society for Psychical Research
4 West 73rd Street, New York
NY 10023

Founded in 1885, it is well-known for its open-mindedness and impartiality as well as for the quality of its research. There is a quarterly Journal, a Newsletter and access to an excellent library. Membership fees vary.

The Parapsychology Foundation Inc.
228 East 71st Street, New York
NY 10021

This organization is unique in that it has no members, but its regular and authoritative *Parapsychology Review* and its valuable contributions to international conferences throughout the world exert considerable influence. It was founded by mediumistic Eileen Garrett in 1951 and for years its annual cash scholarship, its grants for original research and its library of 10,000 volumes have been of inestimable value to the furtherance of practical psychical research and allied subjects.

The Academy of Religion and Psychical Research
PO Box 614, Bloomfield
CT 06002

The Center for Scientific Anomalies Research
PO Box 105, Ann Arbor
MI 48103

The Central Premonitions Registry
Box 482, Times Square Station
New York, NY 10023

The Division of Personality Studies
University of Virginia Medical Center
Charlotteville, VA 22908

The Foundation for Research on the Nature of Man
Box 6847, College Station
Durham, NC 27708

The International Association for Near-death Studies
Department of Psychology, University of Connecticut
Storrs, CT 06268

The Mind Science Foundation
8301 Broadway, Suite 100
San Antonio, TX 78209

The Parapsychological Association Inc.
PO Box 12236, Research Triangle Park
NC 27709

The Parapsychology Institute of America
42–47 78th Street, Elmhurst
New York, NY

The Psychical Research Foundation
Psychology Department, West George College
Carrolton, GA 30118

The Psychical Research Foundation
Duke Street, Durham
NC 27706

The Psychophysical Research Laboratories
301 College Road East, Princeton
NJ 08540

The Spiritual Frontiers Fellowship
10189 Winner Road
Independence, MO 64052

The Institute of Parapsychological Studies
5740 Yonge Street
Toronto, Ontario M2N 5SI

The Spiritual Science Institute of Toronto
801 St Clair Avenue West
Toronto, Ontario M6C 1C2

AUSTRALIA, ASIA AND THE FAR EAST

Australian Institute of Psychic Research
PO Box 445, Lane Cove
NSW 2066

The Indian Foundation for Parapsychology
Andhra University
Waltair, AP

The Japan Psychic Science Association Inc.
No. 161 1 12–12 Kamiochiai
Shinjuku-Ku, Tokyo

AFRICA

The South African Society for Psychical Research
PO Box 23154, Joubert Park
Johannesburg 2044

EUROPE

Institut fur Grengebiete der Wissenschaft-Imago Mundi
Maximilianstrasse 8, Postfach 8
A-60101 Innsbruck, Austria

Institut Metaphysique International
1 Place Wagram
75017 Paris, France

Group d'Etudes et de Recherches en Parapsychologie
8 rue Octave Dubois
95150 Taverny, France

Institut fur Grenzgebiete der Psychologie und Psychohygiene
Eichhalde 12
D 7800 Freiburg, Germany

Associazione Italiana Scientifica di Metapsichica
Via S. Vittore 19
20123 Milano, Italy

Parapsychology Laboratory
University of Utrecht, Sorbonnelaan 16
3584 CA Utrecht, Netherlands

Instytut Wydawniczy Zwiazkow Zawodowych
Towarzystwo Psychotroniczne
ul. Noakowskiego 10 m 54 Warszawa, Poland

Sociedad Espanola de Parapsicologia
Belen 15, 1 Derecha
Madrid 4, Spain

The books likely to be of interest and help to the serious ghost hunter are many and varied and their number increases every year. The study of the right books written by the right people is an excellent way of acquiring knowledge and something like experience in a short time. While not all the books listed here may be regarded as the best books to be read by everyone knowledgeable on the subject, the majority are the best books in the field. Some are of special interest because they represent important local research or concern a particular case – such as Jay Anson's *The Amityville Horror* and *The Bell Witch* by Charles Bailey Bell, neither of which should be taken as the plain and unvarnished truth. Others are personal favourites of many years standing and are tried and trusted friends.

Abbott, G, *Ghosts of the Tower of London*, Heinemann, 1980

Alexander, Marc, *Haunted Castles*, Muller, 1974
  Haunted Churches and Abbeys of Britain, Arthur Barker, 1978
  Haunted Inns, Muller, 1973
  Phantom Britain, Muller, 1975

Anson, Jay, *The Amityville Horror*, Prentice Hall, New York, 1977 and W H Allen, 1978

Atkins, Meg Elizabeth, *Haunted Warwickshire*, Robert Hale, 1981

Baker, A P, *A College Mystery*, Heffer, Cambridge, 1923

Baldwin, Gay, *More Ghosts of the Isle of Wight*, Cowes, 1992

Bardens, Dennis, *Ghosts and Hauntings*, Zeus Press, 1965
  Mysterious Worlds, W H Allen, 1970
  Psychic Animals, Robert Hale, 1987

Bell, Charles Bailey, *The Bell Witch*, Nashville, 1934

Bell, Harry, *Guide to the Haunted Castles of Scotland*, East Kilbride, 1981

Bennet, Sir Ernest, *Apparitions and Haunted Houses*, Faber & Faber, 1939

Boyd, Elizabeth, *A Strange and Seeing Time*, Robert Hale, 1969

Braddock, Joseph, *Haunted Houses*, Batsford, 1956

Bradford, Anne, *Haunted!*, Redditch, 1992

Branden, Victoria, *Understanding Ghosts*, Gollancz, 1980

Brooke, A O'S, *Legends of Bruges*, St Catherine Press, London, 1910

Brooks, J A, *Britain's Haunted Heritage*, Jarrold, Norwich, 1990
  Ghosts and Witches of the Cotswolds, Jarrold, Norwich, 1981

Brown, Christopher, *Haunted Sherborne*, Sherborne, 1975

Brown, Raymond Lamont, *A Casebook of Military Mystery*, Patrick Stephens, 1974
  Phantoms, Legends, Customs and Superstitions of the Sea, Patrick Stephens, 1972
  Phantoms of the Theatre, Satellite Books, London, 1978

Carrington, Hereward and Fodor, Nandor, *The Story of the Poltergeist down the Centuries*, Rider, 1953

Chambers, Aidan, *Ghosts and Hauntings*, Puffin Books, 1973

Chilcott-Monk, J P, *Ghosts of South Hampshire and Beyond*, Southampton, 1980

Christian, Roy, *Ghosts and Legends*, David & Charles, 1972

Clarke, Stephan, *Ghosts and Legends of Monmouth*, Monmouth, 1965

Coates, James, *Photographing the Invisible*, London and Chicago, 1911

Cohen, Daniel, *The Encyclopaedia of Ghosts*, Michael O'Mara, 1989

Cohen, David, *Poltergeists and Hauntings*, Regency Press, London and New York, 1965

    Price and his Spirit Child 'Rosalie', Regency Press, London, 1965

Collins, Bernard Abdy, *The Cheltenham Ghost*, Psychic Press, 1948

Cox, W L and Meredith, R D, *Haunted Cheltenham*, Gloucester, 1982

Coxe, Antony Hippisley, *Haunted Britain*, Hutchinson, 1973

Currie, Ian, *You Cannot Die*, Hamlyn, 1978

Daniel, Clarence, *Ghosts of Derbyshire*, Dalesman Books, Yorkshire, 1973

Davis, Richard, *I've Seen a Ghost!*, Hutchinson, 1979

Day, James Wentworth, *A Ghost Hunter's Game Book*, Muller, 1958

    Essex Ghosts, Spurbooks, 1973

    Here are Ghosts and Witches, Batsford, 1954

    In Search of Ghosts, Muller, 1969

    The Queen Mother's Family Story, Robert Hale, 1967

Dingwall, Eric J and Hall, Trevor H, *Four Modern Ghosts*, Duckworth, 1958

Dunne, John J, *Haunted Ireland*, Appletree Press, Belfast, 1977

Ebon, Martin, *True Experiences with Ghosts*, New American Library, New York, 1968

Eyre, Kathleen, *Lancashire Ghosts*, Dalesman Books, Yorkshire, 1974

    Lancashire Legends, Dalesman Books, Yorkshire, 1975

Fenoglio, M A, *Fantasmi Spettri: E Case Maledette*, Gruppo Editoriale Muzzio, Trento, 1991

Findler, Gerald, *Lakeland Ghosts*, Dalesman Books, Yorkshire, 1979

Finucane, R C, *Appearances of the Dead*, Junction, 1982

Fodor, Nandor, *Between Two Worlds*, Citadel, New York, 1964

    Mind Over Space, Citadel, New York, 1962

    On the Trail of the Poltergeist, Citadel, New York, 1958

Forman, Joan, *Haunted East Anglia*, Robert Hale, 1974

    Haunted Royal Homes, Harrap, 1987

    The Haunted South, Robert Hale, 1978

Fuller, John G, *The Ghost of Flight 401*, Souvenir Press, 1976

Gauld, Alan and Cornell, A D, *Poltergeists*, Routledge & Kegan Paul, 1979

Godwin, John, *Unsolved: The World of the Unknown*, Doubleday, New York, 1976

Goodrich-Freer, Ada, *The Alleged Haunting of B— [Ballechin] House*, Pearson, London, 1900

Grant, Douglas, *The Cock Lane Ghost*, Macmillan, 1965

Gray, Affleck, *The Big Grey Man of Ben MacDhui*, Impulse Books, Aberdeen, 1970

Green, Celia and MacCreery, Charles, *Apparitions*, Hamish Hamilton, 1975

Greenhouse, Herbert B, *In Defense of Ghosts*, Simon & Schuster, New York, 1970

Haining, Peter, *Ghosts. The Illustrated History*, Sidgwick & Jackson, 1974

Halifax, Lord, *Lord Halifax's Ghost Book*, Geoffrey Bles, London, 1936

Hall, Trevor H, *New Light on Old Ghosts*, Duckworth, 1965

Hallam, Jack, *Ghosts of London*, Wolfe, 1975
  Ghosts of the North, David & Charles, 1976
  The Ghost Tour, Wolfe, 1967
  The Ghosts' Who's Who, David & Charles, 1977
  The Haunted Inns of England, Wolfe, 1972

Harper, Charles G, *Haunted Houses*, Chapman & Hall, 1907

Harries, John, *The Ghost Hunter's Road Book*, Muller, 1968

Herbert, W B, *Phantoms of the Railways*, David & Charles, 1988
  The Railway Ghosts, David & Charles, 1985

Hole, Christina, *Haunted England*, Batsford, 1940

Holzer, Hans, *Best True Ghost Stories*, Prentice Hall, New York, 1983
  Ghosts of Old Europe, Dorset Press, New York, 1992
  The Great British Ghost Hunt, Bobbs-Merrill, Indianapolis, 1975 and
    W H Allen, 1976
  Haunted House Album, Dorset Press, New York, 1992
  The Lively Ghosts of Ireland, Wolfe, 1968
  Psychic Photography, Souvenir Press, 1970

Hopkins, R Thurston, *Adventures with Phantoms*, Quality Press, 1946
  Cavalcade of Ghosts, Kingswood, 1956
  Ghosts Over England, Meridian Books, 1953

Hurley, Jack, *Legends of Exmoor*, Exmoor Press, Dulverton, 1973

Hurwood, Bernhardt J, *Haunted Houses*, Universal-Tandem, 1974

Inglis, Brian, *Science and Parascience*, Hodder & Stoughton, 1984

Ingram, John H, *The Haunted Homes and Family Traditions of Great
  Britain*, Reeves & Turner, 1912

Iremonger, Lucille, *The Ghosts of Versailles*, Faber & Faber, 1957

Kristen, Clive, *Ghost Trails of Northumbria*, Birtley, 1992

Lambert, R S, *Exploring the Supernatural*, Arthur Barker

Lamont, Stewart, *Is Anybody There?*, Mainstream, Edinburgh, 1980

Lang, Andrew, *The Book of Dreams and Ghosts*, Longmans, 1897
  Cock Lane and Common-sense, Longmans, 1894

Legg, Rodney, *Mysterious Dorset*, Dorset Publishing, 1987

Leslie, Sir J R S, *Shane Leslie's Ghost Book*, Hollis & Carter, 1955

Lethbridge, T C, *Ghost and Ghoul*, Routledge & Kegan Paul, 1962

Lewis, Roy Harley, *Ghosts, Hauntings and the Supernatural World*,
  David & Charles, 1991

Ludlam, Harry, *The Mummy of Birchen Bower and Other True Ghost
  Stories*, Foulsham, 1966
  The Restless Ghosts of Ladye Place and Other True Hauntings,
    Foulsham, 1967

Lytton, Lord, *The Haunted and the Haunters*, Simpkin, Marshall, 1925

McEwan, Graham J, *Haunted Churches of England*, Robert Hale, 1989

MacGregor, Alasdair Alpin, *The Ghost Book*, Robert Hale, 1955
  Phantom Footsteps, Robert Hale, 1959

MacKenzie, Andrew, *Apparitions and Ghosts*, Arthur Barker, 1971
    Frontiers of the Unknown, Arthur Barker, 1968
    Hauntings and Apparitions, Heinemann, 1982
    The Seen and the Unseen, Weidenfeld & Nicolson, 1987
    The Unexplained, Arthur Barker, 1966
Macnaghten, Angus, *More Berkshire Ghosts and Other Stories*, Slough, 1977
    Windsor Ghosts and Other Berkshire Hauntings, Slough, 1976
Maple, Eric, *The Realm of Ghosts*, Robert Hale, 1964
    Supernatural England, Robert Hale, 1977
Marryat, Florence, *There is no Death*, Psychic Press, London, 1921
Martin, Stuart, *Ghost Parade*, Rider, 1947
May, Antoinette, *Haunted Houses and Wandering Ghosts of California*, California Living Books, 1977
Mercer, T S, *More Thames Ditton Tales and Scandals*, Thames Ditton, 1965
    Tales and Scandals of old Thames Ditton, Thames Ditton, 1965
Meredith, Bob, *Cheltenham, Town of Shadows*, Cheltenham, 1988
Middleton, Jessie Adelaide, *The White Ghost Book*, Cassell, 1916
Mills, Martin G A, *A Trail of Haunted York*, York, 1989
Mitchell, Anne, *Ghosts Along the Thames*, Bourne End, 1972
Mitchell, John V, *Ghosts of an Ancient City*, York, 1975
Moakes, Len, *Haunted Nottinghamshire*, J H Hall, Derby, 1987
Moberly, Charlotte Anne E and Jourdain, Eleanor F, *An Adventure*, Faber & Faber, 1931
Moss, Peter, *Ghosts Over Britain*, Elm Tree Books, 1977
Myers, Arthur, *The Ghostly Register*, Contemporary Books, Chicago, 1986
    Ghosts of the Rich and Famous, Contemporary Books, Chicago, 1988
Nicholls, Jeff, *Our Mysterious Shire*, Slough, 1985
O'Donnell, Elliott, *The Hag of the Dribble and Other True Ghosts*, Robert Hale, 1971
    Ghosts with a Purpose, Rider, 1951
    Haunted Britain, Rider, 1949
    Haunted Churches, Quality Press, 1939
    Haunted People, Rider, 1951
    Haunted Waters, Rider, 1957
    Phantoms of the Night, Rider, 1956
    Rooms of Mystery, Philip Allan, 1931
    Some Haunted Houses of England and Wales, Eveleigh Nash, 1908
Owen, A R G, *Can We Explain the Poltergeist?*, Helix, New York, 1964
Owen, A R G and Sims, Victor, *Science and the Spook*, Dobson, 1971
Oxley, C T, *The Haunted North Country*, Harrogate, 1975
Parish, E, *Hallucinations and Illusions*, London, 1897
Peach, Emily, *Things That Go Bump in the Night*, Aquarian Press, 1991
Pearsall, Ronald, *The Table-Rappers*, Michael Joseph, 1972
Pearson, Margaret M, *Bright Tapestry*, Harrap, 1956
Permutt, Cyril, *Beyond the Spectrum*, Patrick Stephens, 1983
Picknett, Lynn, *Flights of Fancy?*, Ward Lock, 1987

Playfair, Guy Lyon, *The Flying Cow*, Souvenir Press, 1975
  This House is Haunted, Souvenir Press, 1980
Poole, Keith B, *Ghosts of Wessex*, David & Charles, 1976
Price, Harry, *Confessions of a Ghost Hunter*, Putnam, 1936
  The End of Borley Rectory, Harrap, 1946
  Fifty Years of Psychical Research, Longmans, 1939
  Leaves from a Psychist's Case-Book, Gollancz, 1933
  'The Most Haunted House in England', Longmans, 1940
  Poltergeist Over England, Country Life, 1945
  Search for Truth, Collins, 1942
Price, Harry and Lambert, R S, *The Haunting of Cashen's Gap*, Methuen, 1936
Randles, Jenny, *Beyond Explanation?*, Robert Hale, 1985
Redesdale, Lord, *Tales of Old Japan*, Macmillan, 1910
Reynolds, James, *Gallery of Ghosts*, Creative Age, New York, 1949
  Ghosts of Irish Houses, Creative Age, New York, 1947
Rhys, Ernest (ed.), *The Haunters & the Haunted*, Daniel O'Connor, 1921
Rice, Hilary Stainer, *Ghosts of the Chilterns and Thames Valley*, Slough, 1983
Ritchie, Jean, *Inside the Supernatural*, Fontana, 1992
Robb, Rosemary, *Ghost Hunting* (Nottinghamshire and East Midlands), J H Hall, Derby, 1992
Roberts, Nancy, *An Illustrated Guide to Ghosts*, Charlotte, North Carolina
Roll, William G, *The Poltergeist*, Wyndham, 1972
Rosenthal, Eric, *They Walk in the Night*, Allen & Unwin, 1949
Royal, Margaret and Girvan, Ian, *Bristol Ghosts and Their Neighbours*, Bristol, 1977
  Local Ghosts, Bristol, 1976
Ruland, Wilhelm, *Legends of the Rhine*, Cologne, 1937
Russell, Edir, *Ghosts*, Batsford, 1970
St Clair, Sheila, *Psychic Phenomena in Ireland*, Mercier Press, Cork, 1972
St Leger-Gordon, Ruth, *The Witchcraft and Folklore of Dartmoor*, Alan Sutton, 1982
Salter, W H, *Ghosts and Apparitions*, Bell, 1938
Sampson, Charles, *Ghosts of the Broads*, Yachtsman Publishing, 1931
Sergeant, Philip W, *Historic British Ghosts*, Hutchinson, 1936
Seymour, Deryck, *The Ghosts of Torbay*, Obelisk, Exeter, 1990
Seymour, Deryck and Hazzard, Jack, *Berry Pomeroy Castle*, Torquay, 1982
Seymour, Percy, *The Paranormal* (Beyond Sensory Science), Arkana/Penguin, 1992
Seymour, St John D and Neligan, H L, *True Irish Ghost Stories*, Dublin, 1969
Singer, Kurt, *Ghost Book*, W H Allen, 1963
Sitwell, Sacheverell, *Poltergeists*, Faber & Faber, 1940
Smith, Susy, *Haunted Houses for the Millions*, Bell, New York, 1967
Spencer, John, *The Paranormal: A Modern Perspective*, Hamlyn, 1992

Spencer, John and Anne, *The Encyclopaedia of Ghosts and Spirits*, Headline, 1992

Steedman, Gay and Anker, Ray, *Ghosts of the Isle of Wight*, Newport, Isle of Wight, 1977

Steiger, Brad, *Real Ghosts, Restless Spirits and Haunted Minds*, Universal-Tandem, 1968

Stevens, William Oliver, *Unbidden Guests*, Allen & Unwin, 1949

Stewart, Frances D, *Surrey Ghosts Old and New*, Purley, 1990

Stirling, A M W, *Ghosts Vivisected*, Robert Hale, 1957

Sturge-Whiting, J R, *The Mystery of Versailles*, Rider, 1938

Tabori, Cornelius, *My Occult Diary*, Rider, 1951 and Living Books, New York, 1966

Tabori, Paul, *Harry Price: the Biography of a Ghost Hunter*, Athenaeum Press, 1950
Pioneers of the Unseen, Souvenir Press, 1972

Tabori, Paul and Raphael, Phyllis, *Beyond the Senses*, Souvenir Press, 1971

Tackaberry, Andrew, *Famous Ghosts, Phantoms and Poltergeists*, Bell, New York, 1967

Thompson, Francis, *Ghosts, Spirits and Spectres of Scotland*, Impulse Books, Aberdeen, 1973

Thurston, Herbert, *Ghosts and Poltergeists*, Burns Oates, 1953

Travis, Peter, *In Search of the Supernatural*, Wolfe, 1975

Turner, James, *Ghosts in the South West*, David & Charles, 1973

Tweedale, Violet, *Ghosts I Have Seen*, Herbert Jenkins, 1920

Tyrrell, G N M, *Apparitions*, Duckworth, 1953

Underwood, Peter, *Deeper into the Occult*, Harrap, 1975
Dictionary of the Supernatural, Harrap, 1978
Exorcism!, Robert Hale, 1990
A Gazetteer of British Ghosts, Souvenir Press, 1971
Gazetteer of British, Scottish and Irish Ghosts, Bell, New York, 1985
A Gazetteer of Scottish and Irish Ghosts, Souvenir Press, 1973
The Ghost Hunter's Guide, Blandford, 1986
The Ghost Hunters, Robert Hale, 1985
Ghostly Encounters, Bossiney Books, St Teath, 1992
The Ghosts of Borley, David & Charles, 1975
Ghosts of Cornwall, Bossiney Books, St Teath, 1983
Ghosts of Devon, Bossiney Books, St Teath, 1982
Ghosts of Dorset, Bossiney Books, St Teath, 1988
Ghosts of Hampshire and the Isle of Wight, St Michael's Abbey Press, Farnborough, 1983
Ghosts of Kent, Meresborough, Rainham, 1984
Ghosts of North-West England, Fontana, 1978
Ghosts of Somerset, Bossiney Books, St Teath, 1985
Ghosts of Wales, Christopher Davies, Swansea, 1978
Ghosts of Wiltshire, Bossiney Books, St Teath, 1989
Haunted London, Harrap, 1973
Hauntings: New Light on Ten Famous Cases, Dent, 1977

A Host of Hauntings, Leslie Frewin, 1973

Into the Occult, Harrap, 1972

Mysterious Places, Bossiney Books, St Teath, 1988

No Common Task: The Autobiography of a Ghost Hunter, Harrap, 1983

This Haunted Isle, Harrap, 1984

Westcountry Haunting, Bossiney Books, St Teath, 1986

Walker, Danton, *Spooks De Luxe* (or *That Ghost I Saw*), Franklin Watts, New York, 1956 and Dobson, London, 1958

Waring, Edward, *Ghosts and Legends of the Dorset Countryside*, Compton Press, Tisbury, 1977

Watkins, Leslie, *The Real Exorcists*, Methuen, 1983

Watson, Lyall, *Supernature*, Hodder & Stoughton, 1973

Whitaker, Terence W, *England's Ghostly Heritage*, Robert Hale, 1989

Ghosts of Old England, Robert Hale, 1987

Lancashire's Ghosts and Legends, Robert Hale, 1980

Scotland's Ghosts and Apparitions, Robert Hale, 1991

Yorkshire's Ghosts and Legends, Granada, 1983

Wilson, Colin, *Afterlife*, Harrap, 1985

The Encyclopaedia of Unsolved Mysteries, Harrap, 1987

Mysteries, Hodder & Stoughton, 1978

The Occult, Hodder & Stoughton, 1971

Poltergeist!, New English Library, 1981

The Psychic Detectives, Pan, 1984

Wiltshire, Kathleen, *Ghosts and Legends of the Wiltshire Countryside*, Colin Venton, Melksham, 1985

Winer, Richard and Osborn, Nancy, *Haunted Houses*, Bantam, New York, 1979

More Haunted Houses, Bantam, New York and London, 1981

Wood, Robert, *The Widow of Borley*, Duckworth, 1992

Woods, Frederick, *Cheshire Ghosts and Legends*, Countryside Books, Newbury, 1990

Acknowledgements

The author and publishers would like to thank the Fortean Picture Library for photographs reproduced on the following pages: 32 (Andreas Trottmann), 37 (Lars Thomas), 44 (Lars Thomas), 50 (Lars Thomas), 51 (Tony Vaci), 55 (Lars Thomas), 118 (George Kanigowski), 122 (Dr Elmar R. Gruber).

The author would like to express his grateful thanks for co-operation and help in many ways, including the use of copyright photographs and pictures from among others: Ray Armes of Norwich; Associated Newspapers; John Austin of Hollywood Inside Syndicate, California; Michael Bingham; John E Birch; Château et Musée Blois; Chris and Carole Brackley of Complete Video Productions, Banstead; the British Museum; the British Tourist Authority; Robert Buckley; Gordon Carroll; the College of Psychic Studies, London; Robert Cooke, MP; Country Life magazine; Philomena, Lady de Hoghton; the Department of the Environment; Crispin Derby; Charles and Lorraine Doerrer of Rochester, New York; Downing and Daily Express; Gerald Fox, FIMechE; Roger Frewen; the Ghost Club; Charles Gladstone of Fasque; Sheila Gomez of Raffles Hotel, Singapore; Edward Griffiths; Jack Hallam; the Rev. R W Hardy; Dr Vernon Harrison; Hartzel Studio; George Hoare of Theatre Royal, Drury Lane; Sir Westrow Hulse; the Irish Tourist Board; the Jamaica Tourist Board; Andrew Jupp; Shozo Kagoshima of the Winchester Mystery House, San José, California; Albert W Kerr; Steuart Kiernander; Landesbildstelle Berlin; the Rev. Kenneth F Lord; Mail Newspapers plc; S P B Mais and J M Dent & Sons; Marjorie Maple and the Hollywood Cemetery Association; Brenda Marshall; Sheila and Phil Merritt of Santa Clara, California; the Rev. William Y Milne; Philip Moore; the National Trust for Scotland; Lord Palmer of Manderston; Dudley Poplak; Russell Read; Astrid Ruffhead; Lord St Levan; Nigel Scott; the Scottish Tourist Board; Betty Shields; Edward M

Sitzberger of St James Hotel, Cimarron, New Mexico; the Swedish Travel and Tourism Council; Stefanie Teichmann and the German Tourist Office; Chris Thornton; City of Toronto Archives; Trust House Forte; Ben Underwood; Chris Underwood; the United States Travel Services; University College of London; Van Werninck Studio, Montrose; Vaux Breweries; West Surrey Newspapers; Jean Whisker; Sheila White; Reginald J Wickens; Chris Yates; the Yorkshire Humberside Tourist Board; and especially Carey Smith and Colin Gower of Anaya Publishers, for their invitation to write the book, their interest and help throughout its composition and their enthusiasm and confidence at all times. The author is also deeply indebted to his wife for all her help, patience and understanding.

Index

Page numbers in *italic* type refer to illustrations.